Pack Prints

ENG 1013: COMPOSITION II

Campus Writing Program • Second Edition
Department of English, Philosophy, and World Languages
Arkansas State University

Editor-in-Chief
Airek Beauchamp

Assistant Editors
Zach Warzecka
Kerri L. Bennett
Kristi Murray Costello

Editorial Assistants
Leslie Reed
Jonathan Carmack

Editorial Staff
John Abernathy • Tianna Baker • Elizabeth Chamberlain • Helen Duclos •
Robin Everett • Robyn Frost • Bethany Gallimore •
Marie-Jose Patton • Rae Summers-Thompson • Roy Tanksley • Mitchell Wells

Faculty Authors
Rebecca Barrett-Fox • Airek Beauchamp • Kerri L. Bennett • J. Justin Castro •
Jacob Caton • Kate Krueger • Vicent Moreno • Kristi Murray Costello •
Robert Robinette •Sarah Scott • Zack Warzecka • Steven Weimer

Student Authors
Courtney Baker • Colby Cockrill • Karis Evans • Lathan Garnett •
Meagan Hamilton • Garret Harlow • Amber Hatcher • William Kazyak •
Austin May • Seth Price • Gabrielle Rannals • Rae Summers-Thompson •
Joseph Thomas • Patrick Tribbett • Nathan Walters

macmillan learning
curriculum solutions

Printed in the United States of America

10 9 8 7 6 5 4 3 2 1

ISBN 978-0-7380-9434-2

Macmillan Learning Curriculum Solutions
14903 Pilot Drive
Plymouth, MI 48170
www.macmillanlearning.com

Costello 9434-2 F17

Sustainability
Hayden-McNeil's standard paper stock uses a minimum of 30% post-consumer waste. We offer higher % options by request, including a 100% recycled stock. Additionally, Hayden-McNeil Custom Digital provides authors with the opportunity to convert print products to a digital format. Hayden-McNeil is part of a larger sustainability initiative through Macmillan Learning. Visit http://sustainability.macmillan.com to learn more.

bedford/st. martin's • hayden-mcneil
w.h. freeman • worth publishers

Editor-in-Chief
Airek Beauchamp

Assistant Editors
Zach Warzecka • Kerri L. Bennett • Kristi Murray Costello

Editorial Assistants
Leslie Reed • Jonathan Carmack

Cover Artist
Ross Carroll

Layout Editors
John Abernathy • Kerri L. Bennett

Editorial Staff
Helen Duclos

Roy Tanksley

John Abernathy

Robyn Frost

Mitchell Wells

Bethany Gallimore

Marie-Jose Patton

Elizabeth Chamberlain

Tianna Baker

Robin Everett

Rae Summers-Thompson

Faculty Authors
Zach Warzecka

Kristi Murray Costello

Rebecca Barrett-Fox

Robert Robinette

Steven Weimer

J. Justin Castro

Airek Beauchamp

Kerri L. Bennett

Kate Krueger

Vicent Moreno

Jacob Caton

Sarah Scott

Student Authors

Joseph Thomas	"Emotionless: Writing in the Lines"
Karis Evans	"The Importance of Global Journalism"
Austin May	"The Great Debate"
Seth Price	"What Do Standardized Tests Accomplish?"
Garret Harlow	"Agriculture: Saving Civilization"
Nathan Walters	"Will You Settle for the Norm?"
Patrick Tribbett	"Monsters in the Media"
Gabrielle Rannals	"What Americans Lack in Scientific Knowledge"
Amber Hatcher	"Muggles and Mudbloods and Creatures, Oh My! Racism in the Wizarding World"
William Kazyak	"Deception and Destruction: Operation Fortitude and the Allied Aerial Support for Operation Overlord"
Courtney Baker	"Coal Mining: From Providing to Destroying"
Rae Summers-Thompson	"Raiders of the Lost Archives: Researching the 1930 Arkansas v. Wiley College Debate"
Colby Cockrill	
Lathan Garnett	
Meagan Hamilton	

Table of Contents

Table of Contents

Annotated Student Essay   155

Sample Papers in MLA, Chicago, and APA Styles   163

Table of Contents

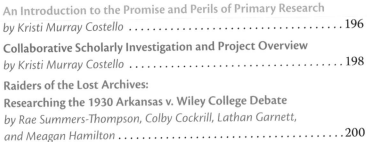

Acknowledgements

A thank you to everyone who has made this possible. I couldn't have done this without the help of the entire Arkansas State University campus. The climate of support for students and the drive to create better writing instruction have allowed my colleagues and me to continually improve the ways we can help students across campus. I would like to thank our students and faculty members who contributed to this volume as well. This, however, barely touches the network of support that has led to this volume.

I need to thank Kerri Bennett and Dr. Zach Warzecka for their tireless editing on this volume. Without their perceptive editing and clear understanding of the purposes and rhetorical underpinnings for this project, I would never have finished. I will never be able to thank you enough.

Faculty and student contributions to this volume have been incredibly helpful. Our faculty works to continually improve our instruction and curriculum as our pedagogies evolve, and because of this, we feel that our students are able to grow much more as writers. Our Composition faculty whose students have been published in this volume include Kerri Bennett, Dr. Marcus Tribbett, Helen Duclos, Dr. Elizabeth Chamberlain, and Geoffrey Clegg. Their support of these students ensured the success of this volume of *Pack Prints*.

The faculty submissions for disciplinary writing and library use are demonstrative of the faculty members' commitment to our students' development as writers and scholars. Many thanks to Dr. Rebecca Barrett-Fox, Drs. Jacob Caton and Steve Weimer, Sarah Scott, Dr. Kate Krueger, Dr. Vicent Moreno, Dr. J. Justin Castro, and Robert Robinette. Your contributions provide our students with great overviews of the fields they are entering. Finally here I want to thank Dr. Ross Carroll for the use of his stunning photography.

I want to thank Dr. Missy Nieveen-Phegley and Wendy Stewart for handing down to me their expertise in putting together such a collection. Missy's *Beyond the Blank Page* was my first endeavor into anthologies of student writing while Wendy's guidance on *Binghamton Writes* was also essential to my development as editor of this volume of *Pack Prints*. Finally, Dr. Kristi Murray Costello's support and mentorship has been fundamental in the success of this series.

Pack Prints has been supported from the beginning by Dr. Janelle Collins and our Associate Dean, Deborah Chappel-Traylor. Through their support, and most recently that of our new Dean, Dr. Carl Cates, we have seen the Writing Program grow immensely over the last three years. I would like to thank Dr. Elizabeth Chamberlain and Dr. Zach Warzecka for their help in the expansion and success of our program. Finally, Lisa Wess and her crew at Hayden-McNeil have also been instrumental in developing this edition, and volume, of *Pack Prints*. I must also thank, again, Dr. Kristi Murray Costello, this time as a mentor *and* a friend. Her wherewithal, drive, and patience are nothing short of exemplary.

Finally, thank you, the reader and student of our First-Year Composition program. It is your dedication to your scholarship and your field that inspired us to compile this publication. Keep this going by submitting your own work to us for the next edition. Best of luck in your endeavors!

Dr. Airek Beauchamp

Lead Editor, Pack Prints Composition II

Assistant Director, Writing Program and Writing Center

Assistant Professor, Rhetoric and Composition

A Note to Readers

In your hands is the second edition of *Pack Prints*, Arkansas State University's anthology of outstanding student writing, but the first edition solely dedicated to Composition II. Our first edition, assembled, written, and edited by Dr. Kristi Murray Costello and Tabatha Simpson-Farrow, was able to be used universally across our first-year composition courses. As our writing program has evolved, so have our pedagogies, and we believe we are now able to focus on each First-Year Writing course individually. At Arkansas State, Composition II is distinctly focused on teaching students to write in the disciplines. In Composition I, you learned genre and rhetorical awareness and became prepared to tackle reading and writing in a variety of contexts. This book picks up where the last left off. You are no longer novice academic writers—you are now on your way to becoming scholars, and this change in your academic identity is reflected in the way this book operates.

We begin this book with an introduction to what it means to be able to read and write at a scholarly level. We are careful to note that we can give you broad advice about reading and writing for the university, particularly regarding skills you gleaned from Composition I. Here we build on broad terms such as rhetoric and genre, and we introduce you to deeper concepts meant to help you learn to read and write specifically for your discipline, whatever that may be. In the first chapter, we cover strategies to familiarize yourself with the discourses and conventions of your discipline, as well as the disciplinary boundaries that define it. While it is impossible to teach students how to write for every disciplinary situation or genre, we aim to provide you with the skill sets you will need for self-instruction. We believe that teaching students to become independent readers and writers is of the utmost importance. As you develop these skills, you will find that you are also a more independent and critical thinker, traits that will serve you well in every aspect of your life.

The skills that you will develop as an independent and critical thinker are the same skills that will enable you to fully engage in your chosen field. Throughout the book, you will find allusions to "the conversations" different disciplines have. One very important step in developing as a scholar is understanding that you are entering an ongoing conversation, and this conversation is decades, and in some cases centuries, old. You will be tasked with the somewhat daunting responsibility of simultaneously becoming familiar with the background of the conversation while also learning to develop your perspectives in and contributions to the conversation. For this we have provided a variety of resources.

In this volume of *Pack Prints*, you will find disciplinary writing guides created by faculty as well as an overview of how to conduct library research and how to cite sources in the various style formats. You will also find samples of assignment sheets written by Composition II instructors at Arkansas State. These, along with the preceding notations from the instructors, will help you better understand the pedagogies driving our assignments. Following this are examples of student work that has been written in Composition II and will provide great models for the writing you will compose in this class.

We have arranged the essays to reflect the scaffolding of assignments in Composition II—that is to say, they are arranged to illustrate how previous or touchstone assignments develop skills, and often actual writing, that aids the author when composing larger assignments. For example, the Analysis of Writing in Your Major asks students to perform a discourse analysis of the scholarly writing in that field, and the Literature Review then asks students to compose a review of relevant literature in their field. These genres build towards larger, more academically focused assignments such as the Argumentative Essay and the Position Paper. As you work through these different examples of student writing, you will notice how the discourse, organization, and conventions change according to genre, audience, purpose, and situation. This new awareness of writing conventions will aid you in modeling your own writing to fit within the appropriate genre. In the interest of transparency, and to help demystify the evaluation criteria we use for assessing student work, we provide you with both the polished draft of an argument essay and an earlier draft of the same essay accompanied by instructor annotations. We have also included an example of visual argument, an emergent form of visual rhetoric that we expect to become more prevalent in the coming years. To help you better visualize the ways in which different style guides work, you can also find sample student essays in MLA, APA, and Chicago formats. Finally, as primary source and archival methods are becoming more valued in writing studies and many other disciplines, we have included an example of a group archival research project from Dr. Kristi Murray Costello's Advanced Composition class.

Our editorial team has deemed each of the essays in this collection to be exemplary, but that is not to say that they haven't been through rigorous revision, coached by writing faculty through the process. While we do see them as exemplary, we also understand, as we hope you do, that they were written to a specific purpose and audience—they were written to satisfy their instructors' requirements. These requirements will shift from instructor to instructor, so while we are proud of the work our students produced, we also know that these essays will leave a space for discussion and critique. We simply ask that in our classrooms, the work in this text be treated with respect, and that it provides fertile ground for lively discussion while also serving as models for the work you will complete.

Above all, our desire is that you find this text to be not only useful, but actually enjoyable. We have crafted it with care, which we hope shows through in the final product.

Airek Beauchamp, Editor-In-Chief

A Note to Readers

A User's Guide to *Pack Prints*—
Composition II:
Writing and Reading Rhetorically

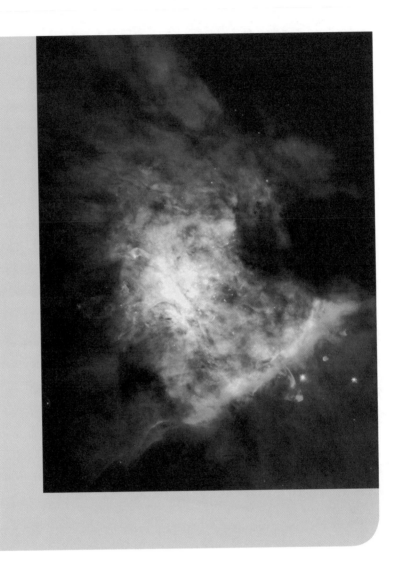

A User's Guide to *Pack Prints*—Composition II: Writing and Reading Rhetorically

Airek Beauchamp and Zach Warzecka

The unspoken premise of this guide is to acquaint students with, and dare we say even teach, writing, particularly writing within the university. *However*, this guide will not, and cannot, teach you *how* to write. Such a goal is impossible given the multivalent nature of Language and Persuasion. This is to say that there is no way to fully codify, predict, and "master" the innumerable writing situations in which you will find yourself. Despite this impossibility, a common goal of writing instruction remains to "train students in academic modes of writing." What a claim! Upon entering the Academy, writers will soon find that academic writing is not a monolithic endeavor; different academic communities call for differing modes of performance to meet the needs of complex and shifting audiences. How could one text prepare you to master the sheer onslaught of variables you will face as a writer?!?

One text cannot prepare you to master any kind of writing, let alone the diverse genres of writing that you will encounter in your particular field. What *this* text can do, then, is serve as a starting place to help you develop and hone your own sense of what your field, and each specific writing situation, will ask of you and how you will, in turn, respond. This endeavor will not entail developing a singular form of writing that will work in every situation. Rather, the goal of this guide is to promote you to read writing situations *rhetorically*, adapting your writing to the needs of situations and audiences with which you are not already familiar. But the ability to adapt to the needs of particular situations must *start* somewhere. After all, one cannot venture into the unknown without first having *something* stable to stand upon. The danger becomes, however, that the stability of a starting point can often be confused with a foundation—as rigid and immutable (a "rule" that must be followed). In what follows, we offer starting points that we hope will promote you to bend, shift, and change to meet the distinctive needs of the (academic) situations you will inevitably encounter.

In plainer terms, we will provide a preliminary guide to academic writing in your field, written by a practicing academic in your discipline. Each disciplinary-specific guide will provide you with an overarching sense of how academics write within their field as well as the more particularized conventions of a common genre in which the members of the discipline routinely engage. Before we get to these preliminary guides, we'd like to take a moment to discuss the counterpart to writing: *reading*. And particularly, we'd like to suggest a few strategies for reading that will help you become a more versatile and effective writer within your discipline.

A RHETORICAL APPROACH TO READING

How do you read a text? Do you focus on the text's argument? Do you highlight key points? Do you skim the article (gasp) for its main idea? Or inversely, do you close read and focus upon specific details rather than attempting to understand the entirety of the text? While each of these approaches hold merit (save for skimming), we would like to provide an alternative approach. We would promote you to read rhetorically. To read rhetorically is not only to read for *what* a text claims, but also to consider *why the author(s) wrote the text the way it is written*—the **genre conventions** that influence the text. This is a very different approach to take toward a text. Using this perspective, rather than solely attempting to cope with what the text claims (the "what" or "how" of the text), you begin to analyze the factors that influence *why* the text appears the way it does. Indeed, gaining an understanding of this *why* might allow you to write in a similar manner.

The first step in questioning why a text is written the way it is involves considering audience. This should strike a familiar chord; invariably questions of persuasion and writing center upon audience. As you read a text, ask yourself these questions: "Who is this text addressing? Who is its intended audience?" The intended audience heavily influences the ways writers perform, as every intended audience carries with them a specific set of *expectations*. That is, audiences have particular needs that they expect a particular piece of writing to fulfill. So when attending to questions concerning audience, consider the needs of a text's intended audience. What do they want from this text, and how does the text, in turn, accommodate those needs? The more clearly you can articulate a text's intended audience, and the expectations of that audience, the more clearly you will be able to adapt to those expectations when it is time for you to write for that audience.

If a particular text always and already responds to the needs of an audience, then we must also consider the *purpose* of a particular text. Attending to the purpose of a text would involve asking, "What is this text trying to accomplish? What is it trying to do to or for its audience?" Many times, we struggle with an unfamiliar piece of writing because we have yet to understand what it is trying to accomplish. If we asked you to write a literature review, and you didn't know what literature reviews *do* (i.e., what they try to accomplish), then you might become quite confused indeed! But if we told you that a literature review summarizes the writings of other writers in order to illustrate where your ideas stand in relation to other people's thoughts, you'd have a much clearer sense of *what this particular piece of writing attempts to do.* Reading for a piece of writing's purpose and developing the ability to recognize the purpose of a text will aid you tremendously moving forward.

Thus far, we've focused upon influences that remain relatively "close" to a text, audience expectations, and the purposes of writing. We'd now like to draw your attention to a larger concept that influences both audience expectations and the purposes of writing: *community.* In academia, we speak of communities as *disciplines.* For our purposes, a discipline is a community of academics who share theories, knowledges, and methods of research—that is, shared ways of creating questions germane to their domains of inquiry and evaluating answers to those questions. To facilitate research, and the distribution (sharing) of research, academics develop recurrent ways of communicating with one another: **genres** (what we've been loosely referring to as "texts" and "pieces of writing" up to this point).

We should pause here and clarify our terms a bit, as we've just introduced a whopper. When you think of the word genre, you might think of categorization, perhaps the way we categorize movies (horror, comedy, romance, etc.). Let's push further beyond this everyday definition. In academic writing, genres refer to the customary ways writers communicate in response to recurrent situations and audiences. Thus, we might consider an analysis as a genre: a piece of writing that addresses a particular (academic) audience, who in turn carries a set of expectations as to how this genre will be written (based upon their needs and values), while also fulfilling a particular purpose (in this case to break down something and show how it works). The thing to be mindful of, however, is that genres are *particularized to the communities within which they operate.* That is, a genre such as an analysis will change depending upon the specific discipline or community that uses it. For instance, an analysis performed within the discipline of Theatre will have a subtly different purpose, set of audience expectations, and conventions than an analysis performed within Rhetoric and Writing Studies. When you find yourself writing a particular genre, consider finding other examples of the way in which writers *within that particular community* perform the genre. This will provide you with a more concrete sense of the specific conventions, purposes, and expectations that the genre meets. As you further pursue your discipline, advancing towards your major, you should notice that often the readings you are asked to digest have many commonalities, not only in language, vocabulary, and organization, but also in how texts provide evidence, how academics construct arguments, and what counts as knowledge. Becoming aware of these disciplinary, or communal, conventions will allow you to begin tailoring your performances to fit within, mirror, and even transform these conventions according to your needs.

Though genres and genre conventions might seem deeply constraining at first—we've spoken quite a bit about accommodating the pre-existing expectations of a genre's audience, purpose, and discipline—it is important to remember that genres and the communities in which they operate remain alive and *always* continue to evolve. This evolution means that disciplines adapt and change as scholars discover knowledge, or introduce revolutionary ideas and methodologies. As a disciplinary scholar, it is important to understand this evolution and to learn when it is advantageous to follow the preceding conventions and when you feel that it is better to break free from them. If you find that, so far, this guide has seemed to prescribe the ways you must write for your discipline, keep in mind that as a scholar, you maintain your own authorial agency. This freedom is tempered by the fact that you must continue to communicate in ways that members of your academic community will find reasonable and valid. We hope that the information you find in the remainder of this text will help you explore both the parameters of your discipline as well as the freedom you have inside of them.

LAYING THE LAND: LAYOUT AND STRUCTURE

As you work your way through this book, you will notice that we have arranged the material to best serve as a guide to the disciplinary writing you will encounter in Composition II. The second chapter is specifically a Writing in the Disciplines guide. The material in this section has been written expressly for students in Composition II at Arkansas State University. In this section, professors from a variety of disciplines have contributed disciplinary writing guides which explain the conventions and discourses particular to their fields. We hope that these essays serve as guides or touchstones as you begin to research and write within your own discipline. Included in this section is a general guide to conducting efficient research, written by one of our librarians. Following this, we have included a third chapter, a guide to formatting your writing according to the different style guides that each discipline employs. We hope you find this text useful in your development as a writer not only in Composition courses but also as a scholar in your field. Once we situate disciplinary writing and the art of research, we move to more concretely contextualized assignments for Composition II.

The fourth chapter in this text contains material provided by instructors of Composition II. Here you will find sample assignment sheets with individual notes about how and why the instructors composed the assignments. The purpose here is twofold: first, we wish to make our driving pedagogical theories more accessible and transparent. We believe that writing instruction, especially as guided by Rhetorical Genre Theory, is best presented laid bare, exposing each and every intention and pedagogical aim. Second, we believe that our choice to include this material might help familiarize you with the kinds of assignments you will find in Composition II so that you know, on the surface, what you might be asked to do. Having provided some example assignments, we will then move to even more concrete examples of the work required in your class.

The fifth chapter contains several examples of student work from Composition II in a variety of genres. Actual examples of student writing from previous Composition II classes are crucial to providing good writing instructuction. Our decision to include this material coincides with our decision to include the material in the previous chapter. It is our goal to make clear the genres, conventions, and discourses you will see in Composition II, and providing student papers as models seems like a logical step toward that goal. We intend these examples to be not only models but sources of class discussion. It is important to note here that though we are providing you with examples and models of the type of work you will find in your Composition II class, you will still need to pay close attention to the rubrics and assignment sheets provided by your own instructor. **Each instructor will provide a nuanced take on the assignment and will privilege certain aspects the assignment is designed to foster**.

Following this we include a brief sixth chapter in which we provide a student essay with the instructor's comments in the margins. These annotations serve to further our goal of transparency and demystifying the evaluation criteria we use to assess grades. The notes provided by the instructor signal ways in which the student excelled at certain aspects of writing according to a specific assignment sheet. The goal of this section is to provide a sort of forensic explanation of what makes student writing successful in Composition II. For further review we have provided the polished draft of this essay in the fifth chapter. Chapter seven provides examples of student writing in MLA, APA, and Chicago styles as models for formatting and integrating sources.

The final chapter features an example of a group assignment in archival research. In many disciplines primary research and archival methods are gaining traction and, as Dr. Costello explains in her introduction to this chapter, this example will be fruitful to students who engage in such work not only as a model of the kind of writing the students performed, but also the limitations and opportunities provided by these research methods.

Writing in the Disciplines

Introduction

As we considered in the introduction, each discipline will have its own set of conventions, discourses, boundaries of knowledge and genres. Learning to read these guiding disciplinary dictums is important to your success as a scholar in your chosen field of study. In this section, we have asked professors from across the A-State campus to provide writing guides that you might follow when engaging in their particular scholarly discourses. We have organized this section to flow as follows:

KATE KRUEGER—"WRITING IN THE HUMANITIES"

- Dr. Krueger breaks down the conventions of literary analysis, revealing the ways in which humanities scholars utilize inductive reasoning to generate novel interpretations of texts.

REBECCA BARRETT-FOX—"WRITING IN THE SOCIAL SCIENCES"

- Dr. Barrett-Fox discusses the methods and responsibilities of scholars in the social sciences, going further to explain the attendant genres, audiences, and overall scope of the social sciences.

VICENT MORENO—"WRITING IN A FOREIGN LANGUAGE"

- Building conceptually upon Dr. Krueger's and Dr. Barrett-Fox's essays, Dr. Moreno addresses artifact analysis across different languages. Dr. Moreno articulates the methods, goals and purpose of the overarching genre of analysis.

STEVEN WEIMER AND JACOB CATON—"A GUIDE TO WRITING IN PHILOSOPHY"

- Dr. Weimer and Dr. Caton move from analysis to argument, forwarding the ways in which philosophers persuade their audiences via well-constructed arguments. They stress clarity, organization, and logical reasoning as fundamental elements of good scholarly writing in Philosophy.

J. Justin Castro—"Writing History"

- Dr. Castro expands on the writing of his colleagues by addressing not only analysis and argumentation but also the formulation of effective research questions—questions that fruitfully guide research. Dr. Castro illustrates the importance of primary research materials in providing persuasive accounts of the past.

Sarah Scott—"Writing for the Field of Communication"

- Sarah Scott moves the discussion to the importance of research in scholarly writing for Communication. Scott shows the rhetorical utility of various style guides in addressing various modes of communication and rhetorical situations.

Robert Robinette—"Library and Information Research"

- Finally, Robert Robinette discusses the library as the nexus of research on the Arkansas State campus. Robinette explains the different ways scholars should use library resources effectively.

Conceptually the writing guides move from analysis to argument, and argument to research, showing the disciplinary conventions that scholarly writers operate within. Remember that the guides provided herein function as just that, *guides*. Scholars did not find disciplinary conventions etched into stone tablets or sprouting from the wellspring of knowledge. It is important to understand disciplines and their discourses and conventions as social constructions that continue to evolve as scholars participate with one another within the conversations of their prospective fields.

Writing in the Humanities

Kate Krueger

Associate Professor of Literature at Arkansas State University

. . . .

When you open a book you must begin with an open mind. Whereas in the sciences you might begin with a hypothesis regarding what you might find in your investigation, in the Humanities we work via inductive reasoning. This means that we have no preset expectations regarding the meaning of the work. Rather, as we read we make observations about structural patterns and other elements of a text. The term "text" here is important; everything is a text. While in literature courses one might focus on novels, and in history classes one might analyze historical documents, in composition courses texts might include advertisements, film, or even fashion. In the Humanities, we understand that textual analysis depends upon our attentiveness to detail and the messages being conveyed by these modes of expression. We examine what we've found and draw conclusions from that information. Those conclusions become the basis of our thesis statements. The last part of our reading experience thus becomes the beginning of the writing process.

Observations are essentially the "what" and "who" of a text. These are concrete details. The argumentation of Humanities writing depends upon a grasp of those "whats," but a basic understanding of those elements is not enough. We also have to explain the "why" and "how." Why are those features significant? How do they contribute to or provide broader insight into the meaning of the text or of the topic as a whole? We must explain the nuance and the importance of the material that we've found because others might read it differently. It is not enough to simply point out where you found patterns. Through your analysis, you show the "why" and "how"— you essentially prove that your interpretation of the information is the correct one. Indeed, another reader may overlook the elements that you see as integral to the text.

As a writer, then, you must first be an observant reader. While there is often no single "correct" answer to textual analysis, this does not mean that every interpretation is equally legitimate. Because texts are complicated systems of communication, there is more than one message being conveyed at the same time. One reader's analysis may provide insight into the representation of social categories such as gender, while another reader might focus on the way in which the writer uses a certain tone. But, if a reader uses deductive reasoning and makes assumptions about what the text is doing without attending to its actual details, or if the reader misreads, misrepresents, or misinterprets the language, then those analyses are wrong. Inductive reasoning and textual analysis rely on a set of observational skills and an understanding of the makeup of a text. It's up to us as teachers to give you the vocabulary to enable you to see the patterns and make astute observations.

When you have made your conclusions and have an argument in mind, you will regularly use three primary elements to convey messages of your own: ethos, pathos, and logos. You will need to know what you think, who you are, and to whom you are writing. This is your "rhetorical situation." In a composition classroom, you will be asked to consider multiple circumstances in which your writing will attempt to convince an audience. Those circumstances will change the way you approach your writing. How will the particular audience of this work be convinced? First, you will have to establish your ethos, which is a set of techniques that convinces others that you are trustworthy and knowledgeable. This can be created in lots of ways, including the formality or informality of your language, the mention of your credentials or life experience, and your tone. For instance, I'm using the words "we" and "you" because I want you to like me (we're in this together). But, I also want to mention that I'm an Associate Professor of English because I want you to respect me (I am an expert in the field). You may use emotional appeals (pathos) to move the readers of a letter to the editor to feel sadness or anger, while in academic writing you might rely on logic and facts (logos). Each of these strategies are vital parts of writing as an act of communication between writer and reader.

Whether you are a first-year student in a composition class or a seasoned literary critic who has published several books, your argumentative writing will contain the same basic elements. Your introduction and thesis statement tell us the topic (the "what" you've been tracking through the text) and your major claim about it (the "why" and "how" this topic is significant). In your papers, this might all occur in the first paragraph; when you read a work of literary criticism, the introduction might be four or even ten pages depending upon the length of the argument as a whole. A critic will introduce you to the background you need in order to understand the topic and its significance. This may include defining important terms (because words can imply lots of different meanings, it's always a good idea to define your terminology in the beginning of an argument). The structure of an argument is called "signposting" because it's giving a reader a sense of direction—where are you going and how are you going to get there? You orient the reader through these types of sentences, which are strategically placed at the beginning or end of paragraphs and subsections, so she doesn't get lost along the way. This is why we need transitions. Topic sentences will make smaller claims that help to build a case that supports the

Writing in the Disciplines

thesis, which is the one big argument to which each paragraph contributes. Conclusions review the minor points that you used to prove your overarching thesis, and leave the reader with a clear sense of why all of this matters.

Writers will also acknowledge the arguments of others who have discussed this topic. Why? Because writing is a conversation in print. The bibliography at the end of a work is not just proof that someone has done their homework; it is also a record of the other people to whom the writer is responding. When you read an argumentative article or book, imagine that the writer is in a room with the other people that she mentions in her text. How do they agree? Why and in what way do they disagree? The writer is actually contributing to a long conversation that happens in print, sometimes over decades. When you write an argument, you are participating in that conversation, too.

Your observations, which you gathered the moment you started reading, have been transformed into a unique analysis that expands our knowledge of the topic. In this way, we become part of an intellectual community committed to critical inquiry. In the Humanities we must be open to texts and to the part each of us can play in our collective pursuit of greater knowledge and understanding. Your voice and perspective matter; your writing does make a difference.

Further Resources

Cain, Patricia. "How to do a Close Reading." Writing Center at Harvard University, 1998, writingcenter.fas.harvard.edu/pages/how-do-close-reading. Accessed 21 Nov. 2016.

Dollar, Mark. "What Makes a Good Literature Paper." *Purdue Owl*, 19 Oct. 2010, owl.english.purdue.edu/owl/resource/618/01/. Accessed 21 Nov. 2016.

Writing in the Social Sciences

Rebecca Barrett-Fox

Assistant Professor of Sociology at Arkansas State University

. . . .

The term "social sciences" includes an expanse of disciplines—anthropology, education, economics, geography, political science, psychology, social work, and sociology, as well as their sub-disciplines such as archeology, linguistics, genetics, criminology, and gerontology, and area and cultural studies like women's and gender studies, sexuality studies, American studies, and African American studies. Within each discipline, researchers may adopt a "soft" or humanities-like approach that focuses on theories and supports its ideas with qualitative data or a "hard" approach that focuses on experiments and supports its ideas with quantitative (that is, numbers-based) data. Whether they employ qualitative or quantitative research methods or use a mixture of both (called "mixed methods"), social science writers, unlike writers in many other fields, often devote more pages of writing to their methods than to their results. Indeed, some social science writing's biggest contribution to the field is not *what* the authors find but *how* they find it. Indeed, entire journals, such as *International Journal of Social Research Methodology*, *Journal of Methods and Measurement in the Social Sciences*, and *Journal of Mixed Methods Research* are devoted to publishing articles just on research methods, and disciplines and subdisciplines in the social sciences likewise have their own journals that publish work that pioneers new methods of data collection and analysis. However they conduct their research, though, and across disciplines and research orientations, writers in the social sciences have responsibilities to three groups of people:

Responsibilities to Research Subjects

By definition, social scientists investigate human behavior rooted in our interactions with others. We ask others to let us examine their lives. In exchange, we promise to protect them from harm as much as possible—including when we write about them. To do that, social science writers must:

1. Subject our research proposal to the scrutiny of others in the field. Before we conduct research on living human beings, we ask an institutional review board (IRB) to review our proposal. Composed of other researchers, the IRB notes any areas of potential harm to research subjects and gives us feedback to improve the research plan.

2. Protect research subjects' privacy as we collect data and write up our findings. We may assign pseudonyms and/or change identifying details about our research subjects, such as the town where they live, so their identities cannot be discerned by readers. We tell our readers that we've made these changes with phrases like *Names and identifying details have been changed to protect research subjects' privacy*. We store our notes on a password-protected computer or in a locked file cabinet. When we are finished with our project, we destroy our notes so the information that we have gathered cannot be used against our research subjects in the future.

Responsibilities to Readers

Social science writing is very popular among general readers. News agencies, for example, include social science correspondents who distill the technical details of social science research into journalistic accounts. Self-help books on a variety of topics—being financially savvier, getting along with your spouse, recovering from addiction, or learning tips for success in college—all rely upon social science. Writers ranging from Malcolm Gladwell (author of five *New York Times* bestsellers, including *Tipping Point*, *Blink*, and *David and Goliath*) to Nate Silver (whose subfield is sabermetrics, the study of statistics in baseball) likewise rely on social science when they write. Social science writers show respect for readers when they:

1. State their conclusions at the beginning, often in an abstract of 100–200 words that precedes the main body of text. Readers want to understand *what* you learned in your research before they invest time in reading about the process of *how* you learned it.

2. Avoid jargon. If technical words cannot be avoided, they should be clearly defined.

3. Include only the level of detail necessary to make and support the main point. If, for example, the race of a research subject is important, you should mention it. If it's not, don't.

4. Don't make claims bigger than their research findings indicate. You might have some guesses or hopes that your results mean more, but any conjecture must be clearly marked as such. For example, if you find that one out of four students in your English 102 class fear writing, this does not mean that 25% of all A-State English 102 students fear writing, that 25% of all students at A-State fear writing, or that 25% of college students across America fear writing. It only means that 25% of your particular classmates fear writing. A sample of 20 students in a single section of a single course at a single university simply isn't sufficient for you to make a larger claim, though it might be a data point that allows you to start theorizing about fear of writing in the college classroom.

Responsibilities to Other Researchers

Social science writers are in conversation with other researchers. They show respect for those whose work they are building on or disagreeing with by citing them, either in APA or Chicago style. (Always check with your professors to see which citation style they prefer!) They work to keep the conversation going by clearly describing their logic and methods. Social science writers show respect to other researchers when they:

1. Articulate how their ideas are similar to or different from other researchers' ideas. This shows that they have read the work of their peers and are willing to consider the perspectives of others, usually in a literature review, a genre that summarizes what has already been written on a topic.

2. Explain their methods in detail. Any researcher who reads your work should be able to repeat your research to verify your results. If you don't adequately describe your methods, future researchers won't know exactly what you did and thus won't be able to repeat your research to see if it still holds true. Your writing should precisely describe who you studied, why you chose them, how you convinced them to join your study, what you asked them to do, how you recorded your data, and how you analyzed it. Describe any tools, such as a survey or list of questions in an interview. If these tools are long, you might include them in an appendix or as a hyperlinked document.

3. Be specific when sharing results, using numbers whenever you can to make your point. If, for example, your research indicates that students who spend more time studying earn higher GPAs, you need to explain how many more hours are necessary for an increase in GPA. And how many points is the corresponding increase? If conducting qualitative research (which does not involve numbers), be specific but not flowery with language. If, for example, you are observing the interactions between mothers and toddlers at the checkout line at the grocery store, it is not enough to characterize their interaction as "positive" or "negative." Instead, provide details about tone of voice, posture, hand gestures, and word choices that mothers use when addressing their young children. Such details help other researchers see if the results of your research might help them understand the problems they are addressing.

Social science writing has a real impact on the world. Lawyers consult it when arguing before courts; lawmakers reference it when deciding on public policy; social workers, teachers, nurses, and others in helping professions consult it when trying to assist clients, students, patients, and others they serve. Parents rely on it when they read articles on how to best potty train a toddler, get an unwilling tween to help with chores, or find the best college for their graduating high school senior. In short, it informs many of the decisions people make every day. Following the basic advice outlined above, you can enter the world of social science writing with confidence.

Writing in a Foreign Language

Vicent Moreno

Assistant Professor of Spanish at Arkansas State University

· ·

We usually think of language as a vehicle to express or formulate ideas, a vessel with which to communicate our thoughts. While this is true, one important aspect that sometimes is overlooked is the fact that our perception of the world, how we see and experience life is very much shaped by the language we speak. This is very much noticeable to anyone who starts thinking and writing in a foreign language: words that encapsulate a particular concept and for which we don't have an equivalent in our native tongue; the idiosyncrasies of the syntax in how sentences are constructed; the nuances in evoking pasts and envisioning futures across verbal tenses.

Despite the linguistic and cultural differences, analyzing a literary work in French, for example, will have a similar purpose as an analysis in English: the interpretation of a text. Alternately, writing the review of a film in English or in Spanish will most likely share a number of requirements and purposes that are not imposed by the language *per se* but by the format and the nature of the assignment (or genre). There are important aspects, basic elements of form and content that remain the same (defined thesis and topic statements, distribution of the text in content paragraphs, going beyond the obvious in our analyses, etc.) regardless of the language in which we write. The knowledge of the principles of what constitutes "good writing," which students have already acquired as writers of English, provides a base for writing in a foreign language.

What follows will give you a few tips and guidelines about how to be a successful writer in a foreign language. As mentioned before, the type of writing and its contents will largely be dictated by the nature of the assignment, but there are certain basic elements that are shared across writings. For the sake of clarity, I'll focus here on the specific writing used in the argumentative analysis of a cultural product (a text, a film, etc.), which is one of the most typical forms of academic writing. First, I will provide some details about format, style, and content, or, in other words, what is expected of an academic paper; second, I will explain key elements for the proper use of language when producing essays and will offer some general and useful tips for writing in French and Spanish; finally, you will find some links with more information about some of the aspects mentioned.

1. Format and Content of an Academic Essay

The ultimate purpose of any argumentative academic paper analyzing a cultural product is to provide an interpretation that goes beyond the obvious, creating a new understanding or reading of it. As such, the most important element is the thesis, that is, what claim you make about the text you are analyzing. The paper, then, will attempt to demonstrate your claim through textual evidence or to put it more bluntly: you need to make your reader see what you mean, convince her. Your thesis statement will have to be as specific and concrete as possible. For example, saying "This paper will analyze the topic of love and its presence in the film" would be too broad; instead, you should narrow it, by focusing on a character or a particular aspect within the film: "In this paper, I will analyze how in this film, the love interests of the protagonist symbolize the ongoing democratic processes that were occurring at the time."

In addition to a well-formulated thesis you must organize your essay in a way that is clear and cohesive. Typically, essays will have a title that is not merely descriptive, but captures the reader's attention, and a structure that will consist of three parts: first, an introductory paragraph in which you state your thesis and lay out the purpose and organization of the paper; secondly, a number of paragraphs linked to the thesis with a distinct focus. These paragraphs will include an opening statement and a transitional statement at the end leading to the next paragraph. Finally, there is a conclusion in which, rather than summarizing, you reflect on your previous analysis and how your findings prove your thesis. Note that the conclusion should not present new material.

2. A Few Notes on Foreign Language Writing for an English Speaker

A key element of writing in a foreign language is to try and think in the target language rather than translating it from English. As you formulate your ideas and compose your sentences, think about structures, vocabulary, or expressions that you already know. Literal translations are almost never a good idea because, while the meaning may come across, the grammar is usually very different, resulting in awkward sentences that a non-English speaker might even have difficulty understanding.

As you write your paper, pay extra attention to concordance. Unlike English, many other Indo-European languages like French, Spanish, Portuguese, and even German, have grammatical gender, which, among other things, means that nouns and adjectives have to "agree." While in English the adjective "tall" would stay the same regardless if you're talking about Sarah or John, in Spanish, you will either write "alta" or "alto" depending on who the person is. Something similar happens with verb conjugations in which the verb ending changes depending on who is performing the action indicated by the verb.

Accent marks are another distinctive trait of many languages that English doesn't have. Because of this, they are easily overlooked in papers, but it is important that you include them when writing in Spanish or French. They are not mere cosmetic elements, but they in fact can change the meaning of a word.

"Faux amis" (in French) or "falsos amigos" (in Spanish), which translates as "false friends" are literally very dubious and you should stay away from them. They refer to words that look almost the same in both languages, but which in fact bear a very different meaning. Consider "constipado" in Spanish, which contrary to what it looks like it doesn't make reference to your bowel's movements (or lack thereof), but simply means you have a cold. As you progress in your learning of a foreign language you will find many more of these and it is always a good idea to double check before writing a word that looks suspiciously similar in both languages.

Use technology to your advantage. All operating systems have the option to customize your input language. By doing that when you write in a foreign language, you'll find it easier to type in accent marks, umlauts, and other international characters that don't appear on the physical keyboard. Additionally, set your word processor's language to the language in which you are writing and turn on the spell-checking option. This will help you tremendously in noticing mistakes while you write.

3. Useful Online References for Writers Writing in a Foreign Language

3.1. MLA is one of the most common styles for citing and writing papers in the humanities and the style used for writing about literature and culture. The Purdue Owl is a very well composed and always up-to-date website that will help you with any questions you have about formatting and style: https://owl.english.purdue.edu/owl/resource/747/01/

3.2. There are many online bilingual dictionaries. Word Reference is one of the most useful and user friendly, with a number of examples and words in context. http://www.wordreference.com/

3.3. The False Friends Dictionary is another useful reference to learn about and identify "false friends." The website is available in Spanish, http://www.falsefriends.eu/en and French, http://french.about.com/od/vocabulary/a/fauxamis.htm

3.4. The American Council on the Teaching of Foreign Languages (ACTFL) sets the standard for foreign language education in most schools in the United States. Becoming familiar with their terminologies and their rubrics will help you become a better writer. https://www.actfl.org/publications/guidelines-and-manuals/actfl-proficiency-guidelines-2012/english/writing

Writing in the Disciplines

3.5. Microsoft Word has several tools to help you write in a foreign language. Learn about them here: https://support.office.com/en-us/article/Customize-language-features-in-Word-2013-and-later-8fec4c7b-150e-4226-8087-d00d5093fade

Also, learn how to change your input language in Windows and Mac:

https://support.microsoft.com/en-us/kb/306560

http://www.macworld.com/article/1147039/os-x/accentinput.html

A Guide to Writing in Philosophy

Steven Weimer and Jacob Caton

Assistant Professors of Philosophy at Arkansas State University

Unlike the fields of English or psychology, there are no widely accepted styles or formats for writing in philosophy. If you took a stroll through our University library and landed in the "B" section of the Library of Congress Classification system (where many philosophy books are located), you would find a variety of styles, formats, and structures.

Despite this diversity, there are a number of helpful general recommendations for writing a successful philosophy paper. First, it is important to remember that writing is about communication. In most cases you will be attempting to communicate a philosophical idea of some kind to your reader. In order to do this effectively, your paper will need to exhibit the following:

(1) Clarity: As best as you can, use ordinary language. When using technical terms, make sure to give a definition or characterization of this new term. Do not obfuscate.

(2) Precision: Help your reader by saying exactly what you mean. If you are attempting to argue that proposition P is true, tell your reader early in your paper that this is your aim.

(3) Conciseness: Simplicity and economy are often virtues in philosophical writing. You may find that you can generate page after page on a subject; but ask yourself, for each sentence, whether this has helped progress the aims for your paper. If not, strike the sentence.

Beyond these general recommendations, there are many ways to structure a successful philosophy paper. In many cases you will need to accomplish the following:

(4) Carefully lay out the major positions taken on your topic. Explain, in your own words and in detail, what those on both (or more, as the case may be) sides of the issue believe and why.

(5) Offer any objections or criticisms that you can think of (or have researched) for *all* of the major positions on the issue.

(6) Develop and defend a thesis. This could be either positive (an attempt to develop and defend a position on the issue), or negative (a critique of one or more of the positions taken on the issue). In either case, you will need to defend your thesis with careful, critical argumentation.

(7) Respond to possible objections to *your* thesis. Anticipate the strongest arguments against your view, and do your best to give reasons why these objections are ultimately not successful.

When laying out the major positions on your topic and when representing your thesis or main argument it is often helpful to describe these arguments in premise-conclusion form. That is, it is often helpful to explicitly list the premises of the argument and the conclusion of the argument. For example,

(i)   All humans are mortal.

(ii) Socrates is a human.

(iii) Therefore, Socrates is mortal.

Explicitly representing arguments in premise-conclusion form is helpful to your reader because they know what you're arguing for (conclusion) and why (premises). Arguing in premise-conclusion form also helps you as a writer because it forces you to focus on the essential elements of your philosophical idea, and it helps you achieve the Clarity, Precision, and Conciseness described above.

Once you've explicitly represented your argument in premise-conclusion form, give a defense of your argument by providing reasons for your stated premises as well as reasons to think that your premises support your conclusion. That is, attempt to convince your reader that your argument is a good argument. This is a great opportunity to bring to bear all you've learned in your logic class!

The above recommendations presuppose that philosophy is about argumentation. As such, many of the recommendations that are appropriate for good argumentation in general are applicable here. For instance:

(8) It is never acceptable to use a fallacy in defending or responding to a claim. Consult an elementary logic or critical thinking textbook for a list and discussion of common fallacies.

(9) Use the principle of charity when discussing opposing views and arguments. When describing a rival view, present the strongest version of that view. When interpreting a passage or argument from another author, give the strongest and most plausible interpretation. To refute a weak version of an argument is not an accomplishment, it is a fallacy (namely, the straw man fallacy).

(10) Be careful with empirical claims. If you make use of empirical claims in your paper, make sure to support your claim by citing a reliable source.

Last, be sure to properly cite all work that you quote, paraphrase, or draw from. Two rules of thumb: (i) if the idea didn't come from you, cite the source, and (ii) when in doubt, cite the source. Citation is about giving proper credit to the source of an idea.

Writing History

J. Justin Castro

Assistant Professor of History at Arkansas State University

There are the humanities. There are the social sciences. And then there is history. Like literature, philosophy, and theatre, history has been around since people have been telling stories. In written form, histories are almost as old as writing itself. The discipline, however, took its current form alongside the social sciences in nineteenth-century Europe. Since then, history has borrowed heavily from its cousins in the humanities and the social sciences, taking from each while never fitting completely into either. Unlike most social scientists, historians tend to write narrative stories. The best of them read very much like a good short story or novel. We want the public to be able to enjoy and comprehend our work, even if not as many people read it as we would like. But historians differ from novelists and authors of other forms of fiction in that historical works are nonfiction and are more often than not argumentative and based on a thesis backed by empirical evidence. Historians argue that there are facts and objective truths, and that a serious study of the past can benefit humanity's present and future. It is this empirical component that historians take from the sciences. The fact that we make argumentative cases based on substantial but imperfect evidence is similar to law.

Historical writing varies considerably depending on the medium, individual style, and school of thought, but my goal here is more to provide some nuts and bolts for writing a successful undergraduate history paper than to explore the nuances of style or the philosophy of history. What I am about to suggest, I admit, is a bit formulaic, but I think my advice will prove useful for those of you delving for the first time into the world of professional history. After all, you must nail down the basics before soaring to new heights. So, here are the essentials: come up with a viable question, conduct historical research, compose a strong thesis, and write with clear prose and organization.

Selecting a viable research question sounds easy enough, but it can be difficult and time consuming. It is, in many ways, the most important step toward writing a good paper. The question cannot be too broad to answer in a brief essay. It also can't be so esoteric that there are too few sources. You must be sure your question fits within the parameters of your class and that you have access to sufficient sources. For example, a question far too broad and problematic would be: Why did Germany lose World War II? There are too many variables to comprehend within a semester of study. To

Writing in the Disciplines

write a serious and successful essay or book would require that you at least read German, Russian, and French in addition to English. Would you have access to all the necessary German sources? How do we know the outcome of World War II would have been different if German military leaders had made different decisions? There is no way to know for sure. You can write about World War II, but you will need something much more tangible and specific.

As a history student, you have to be aware of the limitations and opportunities within the sources available to you. History is a slave to evidence, especially primary sources—those sources from the period, place, and people you are studying. That is not to say that historians automatically take sources at face value; we do not. Indeed, you will have to develop two other essential skills on your path to mastering historical writing, the capability to contextualize and the ability to spot biases. Despite all the obstacles and potential pitfalls of comprehending material evidence, history requires proof.

Crucial to finding that goldilocks topic is understanding what sources you have at hand: get to know your librarians, talk to your professors, ask the people that can help you for assistance, and do so now. Many sources can be found in Arkansas State's library databases, including the American Antiquarian Society Historical Periodicals, American Historical Newspapers, and Congressional Publications. There is also an impressive historical archive on the seventh floor of the Dean B. Ellis Library building. Secondary sources, which are more current scholarly accounts in journal articles and books—and which are crucial for understanding your subject and contextualizing your primary sources—are on library shelves, available through inter-library loan, and in databases such as JSTOR and EBSCOhost.

Now, let's go back to developing that research question. After some exploration, you'll find that there are online university databases and microfilm holding historic Arkansas newspapers. There are local sources about World War II in the archive, including letters to congressmen and conversations with German prisoners of war in Arkansas. So, a better question might be: How did residents of northeast Arkansas perceive people of German descent during World War II? It would be a more original topic and there would likely be good materials from which to mold an argument.

Once you obtain a grasp on your sources, you can begin to form your thesis. A thesis states what you are arguing—the point of your paper. In history classes it is important to state the answer to the question that drove your investigation and to place that answer up front in your essay, usually within the first couple paragraphs. Your thesis, once formed, will then dictate much of your paper's organization. This is why the thesis is absolutely critical. It not only states your argument, it lays out how you will argue it. To continue with our hypothetical World War II example, a thesis might end up being something like this: "During World War II, many residents of northeast Arkansas displayed contempt for Germans, but the interaction of local white landowners and German prisoners of war created sympathetic ties between the two populations based on shared notions of hard work and perceived racial similarities." I don't know if this is what the evidence would actually show, but, for now, let's pretend.

This thesis provides a roadmap for your essay. Using secondary sources, you will need to provide some contextual information about northeast Arkansas and World War II, especially about the war with Germany and German prisoners of war camps in Arkansas. You will then lay out the evidence you found, perhaps in personal letters and local newspapers, about contempt for Germans. Then you will explore how interactions between white landowners and German prisoners built mutual sympathies, first through conceptions of work, and then through thoughts about race. Perhaps you uncovered most of this evidence in the archive. Your essay will end with a conclusion that reinforces your argument but also stresses the big picture-significance of your essay. Does it say something about race relations more broadly or the complexity of wartime sympathies in local communities? Maybe there are connections between Germans and residents of northeast Arkansas that still exist today. This is where that broader contextualization is important. It will take considerable study and observational skills. Time is essential to history, to its content and its construction.

Lastly, write with intention and revise your work. Love every word. Make sure your topic sentences are clear and that they relate to their paragraphs. Vary your sentence length and style, but, in general, write concisely and boldly. Check your work for common errors and have other people provide feedback if possible. It is a common mistake for students entering college to think that history is about memorizing dates, facts, and famous people, but it is much more than that. History is about empathy and understanding our place within the context of space and time. History is about storytelling. History is about sleuthing and using well-researched evidence to construct superbly written argumentative essays. For those of you up for the challenge, history can be an eye-opening and rewarding practice.

Writing for the Field of Communication

Sarah Scott

Instructor of Communication at Arkansas State University

Writing in the Disciplines

Humans are storytelling creatures. Sharing and telling stories is unique to the human experience. To be an effective communicator, it is imperative to be a good storyteller. The field of communication is comprised of students and scholars who use and tell stories to meet a variety of needs. As one of the youngest disciplines on many college campuses, the field of communication is interdisciplinary—meaning that research and scholarship cross borders and borrow concepts from many other traditions, including, but not limited to, history, English, sociology, philosophy, and psychology. The result is a dynamic and diverse field that transcends rigid boundaries to look at the many and varied ways humans communicate.

At Arkansas State University, for instance, the classes in communication, and consequently the faculty who teach them, may have a media, journalistic, strategic communication, social science, interpretative, or rhetorical approach. In contrast to fields where there is a uniform approach to scholarship and writing—such as writing in accordance to the Modern Language Association guidelines for English or in accordance with the American Psychological Association guidelines for psychology—scholars and students in communication do not have a definitive standard. The challenge then, for the communication student, is to know the conventions and expectations for the particular area of communication in which they are working. Most often in an undergraduate class, the course instructor will set clear expectations for the type of writing that is expected, but it is a good idea to know the various styles of writing, as well as when and why to use a particular style. The three most common styles of writing used in communication are: 1) Associated Press, 2) American Psychological Association, and 3) Chicago. Here is a brief discussion of each style, how it affects the way the story is told, and what sub-disciplines might utilize that particular style.

Associated Press

The Associated Press (AP) develop guidelines for writing news content. News writing goes well beyond traditional print newspapers. News outlets may include print, television, online, and multimedia news outlets. However, the AP style is often used in public relations and advertising, in addition to journalism, and expands into more current outlets such as blogs and social media platforms. The AP style should be used anytime providing timely, accurate information to a specific audience is the primary goal. Therefore, AP style is not used in scholarly publications. Creating content for news outlets requires writers to be clear, consistent, correct, and concise. In order to achieve the most effective writing in AP style, the inverted pyramid style of organization is used for news writing.

The inverted pyramid may seem to contradict everything you have been taught about narrative writing. However, with news writing, as opposed to most types of writing, the introduction is not a slow build-up to a synthesizing thesis statement. The first sentence of news writing is the lead and the lead contains the most important information the audience needs to know. The who, what, when, where, and why should be covered as concisely and accurately as possible in this lead sentence. One of the ways to think about news writing is to imagine an audience and how they will read a piece of writing. Whether the writing is a news article, a social media post, or a press release, assume that the audience may not read past the first few sentences. If that is the case, did the audience receive the most important information? With the inverted pyramid, the information in the writing proceeds from most important to least important. This style assures your audience receives the most pertinent information of the story first.

You will use AP style any time you are creating news content. Media, journalism, public relations, and advertising classes at Arkansas State University utilize the AP style.

When creating academic writing, however, the AP style is never used. Instead instructors and students will utilize one of the formats of academic writing. Many disciplines, such as sociology, business, nursing, and psychology will use APA style documentation. Many in the field of communication use this style as well.

American Psychological Association

While the name may seem deceptive, the American Psychological Association (APA) is simply one type of documentation that can be used for academic and scholarly writing. Many scholars outside the field of psychology also use this style. Organization, writing style, and reference citations are priorities of APA. One benefit to using APA style is that readers see similar organizational patterns and source citations across readings. This minimizes confusion on the part of readers by allowing readers to focus on the main ideas expressed in the writing. In communication, this style is primarily used by those writing in media and communication studies, and it is suited for both quantitative and qualitative work.

Students and scholars using APA style writing in media or communication studies can find comfort in an easily identifiable format for academic writing. To avoid bias in writing, APA style avoids using first names in writing—to avoid revealing a person's sex. This style also attempts to remove bias concerning race, disability, and sexuality in writing. Gender-neutral pronouns are used when possible. These conventions are strategic choices in an attempt to write as free from bias as possible. In APA style, in-text citations are used with an author's last name and date of publication. Writing in APA style is always done in past tense. For instance, "A. Smith (1999) stated that...." This is a social science approach to communication. Scholars and students who are social science-minded are practicing the scientific study of human communication and human relationships. To that end, the research reads much like that from other fields of science.

Quantitative (objective) research in communication tries to generate information about some aspect of communication phenomenon (answer some communication question) that is generalizable to a larger population. These researchers may utilize survey or poll data to do the analysis. Qualitative (interpretive) researchers in communication are not seeking generalizable data, necessarily, but rather are looking for a more specific and in-depth answer to the communication question asked. Qualitative researchers may use focus groups, case studies, or interviews to gather data. Most students and researchers will find, after taking classes in different styles, a style in which they feel most comfortable.

Communication classes where you might expect to write using APA style include media, research methods, interpersonal communication, and health communication classes. The APA style of documentation is one of the most common in academic writing in the United States. Writing stories in APA style requires creating an effective, scientific argument that is as free from bias as possible. Students will find that they will utilize APA style for a variety of classes during their undergraduate experience at Arkansas State University. However, there is one more style that is found in the communication field at the university, and that is Chicago style.

Chicago Style

Chicago style documentation will be seen most often in the fields of history and rhetoric. Rhetoric is a sub-discipline of communication studies that focuses on persuasion. Chicago's notes and bibliographic style use footnotes or endnotes to contain source citations. This makes the writing easy to read with minimum in-text distractions. The benefit to this style is that unconventional source material may be used that does not have an appropriate citation method in APA. Footnotes and endnotes also allow for authors to include additional information that may seem out of place in the body of the text. Chicago style writes in the present tense and includes author's first names and affiliations, "Angelia Smith, a feminist philosopher, claims...." Author information is included in full because Chicago style recognizes that gender, race, nationality, sexuality, and the like are positive starting points for research for many scholars. Students and scholars in this sub-discipline realize that research is never free from bias. Instead of attempting to remove bias, authors utilizing this style embrace the uniqueness of each individual writer and acknowledge the potential biases instead of trying to avoid them.

Chicago style documentation is used for rhetorical analysis in communication studies. Rhetorical scholars and students attempt to tell a story about why some aspect of communication is or is not persuasive or how language and communication function to persuade. Classes in communication studies where a student might use Chicago style documentation include communication theory, research methods, communication criticism, and rhetoric classes.

While having several styles of writing available may, at first, seem confusing, it is useful to be able to find the right style that best suits the needs of the writer. Knowing the purpose of the writing is a crucial step in picking the correct writing style. And finding the best suited writing style will help any student tell an effective story.

Library and Information Research

Robert Robinette

Student Success Librarian at Arkansas State University
. . . .

"I don't use the library. I never need it."
—Bertha Bumpkin, sophomore Bellybutton Studies major

This type of comment frustrates librarians, but it has some truth to it. You can hop on Google, misspell a few words, and instantly have millions of results on any topic imaginable. The problem, of course, is that much of what you find is worthless. We are inundated with "fake news," propaganda, disguised advertisements, infotainment, and other misleading or inaccurate sources. In a 2016 Stanford University study, more than 80% of students were unable to identify a story prominently labeled "sponsored content" as an advertisement (Stanford 10). Surrounded by constant social media updates, app notifications, and a 24-hour news cycle, students often fail to take advantage of the library's invaluable research tools and quality information sources. Thus, in this section, you will learn about trustworthy, high-quality information sources available to you through the library.

Scholarly Sources

You will hear the term *scholarly* a lot in college, usually in the context of *scholarly journals*, also known as *academic*, *peer-reviewed*, or *refereed* journals. Scholarly journals contain articles written by expert scholars (usually somebody with an advanced degree in the field) for other expert scholars. These articles almost always undergo peer-review, i.e., they are chosen for publication by other experts in the discipline.[1] They also provide extensive documentation of their sources, i.e., they have a bibliography listing their sources. Along with these key features, scholarly journals typically have one goal in mind: contributing new knowledge to a discipline. Scholarly sources may possess other attributes—for instance, they might use technical language or jargon, assume you have background knowledge of the topic, or use discipline-specific research methods—but these will vary from discipline to discipline. You can find scholarly journal articles and other quality sources by searching the library's many research databases.

---

1 A discipline is another term for a field of study, e.g., Biology or Political Science.

Research Databases

The A-State library subscribes to hundreds of research databases that provide access to thousands of information sources, including scholarly journals, e-books, government documents, research reports, and more. Research databases come in a few primary types:

- *General databases*, such as JSTOR, provide sources from a wide variety of disciplines in a wide variety of formats.

- *Specialized databases* focus on a specific discipline or set of disciplines. For example, ABI/Inform focuses exclusively on Business sources.

- *Aggregated databases* such as OneSearch and ProQuest Central are very large databases that collect several databases into one searchable interface. These are often the best places to begin your research because you can almost always find something on even the most esoteric topic.

Most information research will require you to search several databases, so if you do not find what you need in one database, try another—we have plenty.

If you use the library, you will never have to pay for access to information! Even if we do not immediately have access to something you need, we can request it from another library for free by using a service called *Interlibrary Loan.*

For some assignments and projects, professors might require *primary sources*, which are information sources without any layer of analysis or interpretation over them. A *secondary source* comments on, critiques, or otherwise analyzes a primary source. In history and other humanities disciplines, primary sources refer to information sources from the time being studied, e.g., a firsthand account of an earthquake. In the sciences, primary sources typically refer to original research articles, e.g., a report on a study of mutant barnacles. Where you search for primary sources will depend on the discipline in question and your research needs. You might use the library's primary resources databases or the library catalog, which is the searchable interface for everything the library owns. You might even need to dig a little deeper and use the university archives, which is where we store and preserve rare and fragile research materials.

Conducting Effective Searches

Knowing how to access quality library sources is great, but if you struggle to formulate an effective search, you will never find what you need. Here are some quick tips to improve your searches:

- *Search, search, and search again*: Your first few searches will probably be clumsy and demonstrate your lack of knowledge. As you find

Writing in the Disciplines

new sources and learn more about your topic, you will discover new terms to use and new avenues of research to explore. Trying a different search strategy never hurts.

• *Be specific, but not too specific*: Searching for *medical marijuana* is too broad. Searching for *medical marijuana Arkansas children autism garbanzo beans* is probably too specific. You must strike the right balance.

• *Use Boolean search operators*: The *OR* operator will expand your search (useful for synonyms, e.g., *medical marijuana OR medical cannabis*), the *AND* operator will narrow your search, and the *NOT* operator will exclude certain terms. An effective search commonly uses a combination of Boolean operators.

• *Search for specific phrases*: Most databases will allow you to search for a specific phrase by placing it in quotation marks. For example, "*medical marijuana*" retrieves results with that exact phrase whereas *medical marijuana* might give you results on medical devices and growing marijuana but nothing about the concept of "medical marijuana."

• *Use search limits*: You often find too much information. When this happens, it can be helpful to set search limits. You might set a limit for a specific date range, material type, language, or discipline. Setting limits generally provides a more manageable set of results.

Sometimes you search and search and search to no avail. If you struggle to find what you need, contact a librarian to help get you on the right track.

The Physical Library

As an undergraduate, you can check out up to twenty of the hundreds of thousands of books, films, government documents, maps, games, and other sources in the library, all of which can be located via the library catalog. In addition, the library contains:

• Dozens of computers located throughout the library;

• Several printers to use for free printing;

• 23 study rooms, many with whiteboards (you can check out markers from the service desk);

• A presentation room with a projector;

• Innumerable nooks and crannies to hole up in;

• Librarians and library staff with sweet dance moves who can help you with your research.

The library is a welcoming, inviting place with an atmosphere highly conducive to research and creativity. We hope to see you around.

Conclusion

Just as each discipline will have its own set of conventions (as demonstrated by the previous disciplinary style guides) so will each course you take (be it a Gen. Ed. course or a course specifically for your field). As such, Composition II, as taught on the A-State campus, does not follow a set curriculum—that is, not all instructors will teach the same lessons and assignments the same way. It is up to you to adapt to the particulars of the Composition II course you find yourself within. Indeed, your adaptation to Composition II will in many ways mirror your work of adapting to the writing within your larger scholarly career.

In the next chapter, Dr. Kristi Costello and the team at Hayden-McNeil provide you with a guide to citation in the various style formats. As Sarah Scott discussed at length, each style is crafted by experts in the disciplines to fulfill specific rhetorical purposes. Citation is not just a means of making sure you aren't accused of plagiarism; citation also demonstrates your awareness of the mechanisms that drive the scholarship in your disciplines. Clear and correct citation practices help develop your ethos as a scholar in your field. As such, it is important to pay attention to the rules and understand why they are in place.

Citing in the Disciplines

Kristi Costello

Assistant Professor of Composition, Rhetoric, and Writing Studies at Arkansas State University

. . . .

WHEN AND WHY WE CITE

You have likely heard a collective groan anytime the professor at the front of the room explains that the paper she's just assigned needs to be in a specific style, such as APA (American Psychological Association), AP (Associated Press), CMS (Chicago Manual of Style), MLA (Modern Language Association), or Turabian, but universities require students to cite sources for several reasons:

- To give credit to others for their ideas;
- To provide information to readers so they can find the sources themselves;
- To lend credibility to the author's claims;
- To distance themselves from someone else's ideas.

While it is a good practice to give credit to anyone whose words or ideas you share, it is especially important in institutions of higher learning because faculty and students are held accountable for their work. In higher education, one's writing and research can help them obtain publication, tenure, grants, and prestige. However, more importantly, when shared with others, one's ideas, writing, methods, and research can lead to new and improved ideas, writing, methods, and research. This process of sharing and building on one another's ideas has led to life-changing scientific advancements, new perspectives on canonical texts, policy reforms, and social and political movements. In Kenneth Burke's *The Philosophy of Literary Form*, he describes this process as an ongoing conversation. He writes:

> Imagine that you enter a parlor. You come late. When you arrive, others have long preceded you, and they are engaged in a heated discussion, a discussion too heated for them to pause and tell you exactly what it is about. In fact, the discussion had already begun long before any of them got there, so that no one present is qualified to retrace for you all the steps that had gone before. You listen for a while, until you decide that you have caught the tenor of the argument; then you put in your oar. Someone answers; you answer him; another comes to your

defense; another aligns himself against you, to either the embarrassment or gratification of your opponent, depending upon the quality of your ally's assistance. However, the discussion is interminable. The hour grows late, you must depart. And you do depart, with the discussion still vigorously in progress. (110–111)

Thus, if you think about knowledge and the generation of knowledge as unending conversation, it becomes clear that everyone who had a voice in the conversation deserves to be heard and know they were heard. Even when we're refuting their ideas, research, or methods, they still deserve credit for being a part of the conversation because it may have been their finding or mistake that led to the next improvement or advancement. It is also equally important to interrogate the conversation, asking yourself whose voices have been left out and why.

In sum, any time you bring someone else's ideas or work into your writing, you should cite the source. The only time you need not cite is when the information is common knowledge. For example, you would not need to cite that Thomas Jefferson was the third president of the United States of America, but you would want to cite that President Jefferson gave of more than 6,000 of his own books to replenish the Library of Congress after arson perpetrated by British soldiers depleted the library's holdings ("10 things you didn't know about Thomas Jefferson"). When in doubt as to whether information should be cited, cite it. It is always better to over-cite than under-cite. To see essays formatted according to each style guide, please see the examples provided for you later in the book.

· ·

WRITE about an instance in which someone was accused of plagiarism. It can be your own experience or that of a friend, politician, or celebrity. What do you recall about the story? Was it plagiarism? How did people react? What impact did the allegation have on the accused?

· ·

Works Cited

"10 things you didn't know about Thomas Jefferson." *The Washington Post*, 30 June 2011, www.washingtonpost.com/lifestyle/kidspost/10-things-you-didnt-know-about-thomas-jefferson/2011/04/12/AGGLlWsH_story.html?utm_term=.03d87ec3f8a9#comments. Accessed 6 Feb. 2017.

Burke, Kenneth. *The Philosophy of Literary Form*. University of California Press, 1941.

MLA Style

The Modern Language Association of America, or MLA, developed a style guide to establish rules and bring consistency to written academic works. The *MLA Handbook* is most often used in the language arts and humanities disciplines, including literature, literary criticism, English studies, and cultural studies. The most recent publication, the 8th edition, was published in 2016.

MLA GUIDELINES FOR FORMATTING PAPERS

An MLA essay follows formatting guidelines:

- The essay should be typed, double spaced in 12-point font size without additional spacing between paragraphs, in an easy-to-read font (such as Times New Roman) on 8.5-inch by 11-inch paper, with 1-inch margins on all sides.

- Do not include a title page unless required to do so. The first page of the essay should include the author's name, instructor's name, course information, and the date the essay is due. This information should be double spaced and placed in the upper left corner of the page, beginning one inch from the top.

- The title should follow the author and course information and should be centered, in title case (uppercase and lowercase letters), with no underlining, italicizing, or bolding.

- Starting on the first page, each page should have a running header in the right corner, 1/2 inch from the top margin and flush with the right margin, which includes the author's last name and the page number.

- Use the tab key or your ruler to indent the first line of each paragraph 1/2 inch from the left margin.

- Use only one space after periods or other punctuation marks.

- Commas and periods go inside the quotation marks, not outside: "Chapter 1," rather than "Chapter 1", for example.

- Use em dashes (—) and ellipses (…) and replace hyphens (-) with en dashes (–) where appropriate, and make consistent.

MLA General In-Text Citation Rules

Including source information in parentheses after a quote or paraphrase is known as parenthetical citation, and is required when using MLA style.

In MLA, it is important to provide a lead-in or introductory phrase for source quotations, paraphrases, or summaries in the text, especially the first time the source is used. Lead-ins introduce the sources to the audience and provide a smooth transition from the student author's writing to quotes, summaries, and paraphrases within the text. When the author's name is mentioned in the signal phrase, you do not need to include it in the in-text citation, rather use the page number alone, if the source is paginated. However, you will need to continue to include the author's last name in subsequent uses.

Example: Introducing Sources with a Lead-In

As Glenn and Ratcliffe explain in *Silence and Listening as Rhetorical Arts*, we "can more productively discern and implement actions that are more ethical, efficient, and appropriate when all parties agree to engage in rhetorical situations that include not only respectful speaking, reading, and writing, but also productive silence and rhetorical listening" (3).

In-Text Citations: Print Sources

A Work by a Single Author
The author's last name and the page numbers (when available) from the source material should appear in the text. The relevant page numbers appear in the parenthetical citation, not in the text.

Examples
Shor argues that basic writing is "a containment track below freshman comp, a gate below the gate" (94).

Basic writing is "a containment track below freshman comp, a gate below the gate" (Shor 94).

Block Quotations

Begin quotations more than four lines in length on a new line that is indented one inch from the left margin. Place the whole quote, double spaced, within the new margin. Do not use quotation marks. Note that the parenthetical citation comes after the end punctuation.

As a builder, Lubbers was tasked to determine the most effective method for ensuring the safety and integrity of structures in a variety of climates. Lubbers's study found the following:

> The prevailing wind being forecast for January 2 will be from the southwest, and will reach speeds of up to 50 miles per hour. This wind has the potential to cause significant damage to the current construction. The building should be braced heavily to avoid collapse. (202)

Unknown Author

When the author is not known, use an abbreviated title of the source in the parenthetical citation. Use quotation marks for titles of short works (articles, chapters, episodes, songs) and italics for titles of longer works (movies, books, television shows), and include a page number.

The results of the study on multitasking showed that switching from one task to another actually takes more time than giving attention to one task at a time ("Is Multitasking More Efficient?" 6).

Authors with Same Last Name

If two or more cited authors have the same last name, include both authors' first initials. If different authors share the same first initial, provide the authors' full names.

Although some researchers have found that multitasking is actually counterproductive and inefficient (K. Jones 12), more and more students are employing multitasking in their daily lives (P. Jones 46).

Two Works by the Same Author

To cite two or more sources by the same author, include the title (or abbreviated title) in the parentheses, preceding the page number.

Bartholomae states that to be successful, college students must invent a language they feel places them in the realm of academia ("Inventing the University" 146), and argues that basic writing programs both preserve and attempt to bridge cultural differences in the classroom ("The Tidy House" 87).

A Work by Two or Three Authors

If a source has two or three authors, provide the authors' last names in the text or in parentheses.

Collins and Blum outline the way socioeconomics and politics outside the university also play a role in instigating the division between "basic" and "normal" writers (14).

The authors outline the way socioeconomics and politics outside the university also play a role in instigating the division between "basic" and "normal" writers (Collins and Blum 14).

A Work by More than Three Authors

For more than three authors, include the first author's last name followed by et al., or give the last name of each author.

Cincotta et al. assert that the launch of Sputnik expanded the competitive arena between the U.S. and the Soviet Union (68).

Historians assert that the launch of Sputnik expanded the competitive arena between the U.S. and the Soviet Union (Cincotta et al. 68).

Cincotta, Brown, Burant, Green, Holden, and Marshall assert that the launch of Sputnik expanded the competitive arena between the U.S. and the Soviet Union (68).

Indirect Sources

It may sometimes be necessary to use a work that has been cited in another source. For such indirect or secondary sources, use "qtd. in" to indicate the primary source.

According to Harvey Graff, "We do not know what we mean by literacy" (qtd. in Lunsford 252).

Encyclopedia/Dictionary Entry

Use the term being cited in quotation marks for the parenthetical citation of this type of source.

A citation is a "quotation from or reference to a book, paper, or author" ("Citation").

Electronic Sources

For electronic sources, include the first item (author name, title, etc.) in the Works Cited entry that corresponds to the citation.

Do not include URLs in the text unless absolutely necessary; if included, make the URL as brief as possible, such as npr.org rather than http://www. npr.org.

Web Site

A similar study determined that subjects lost more time when switching from a familiar task to an unfamiliar task ("Is Multitasking").

Film

Big Fish, directed by Tim Burton, details the extraordinary life of Edward Bloom (2003).

Television

In *Criminal Minds*, a suspect awakens from a coma with no memory of having committed the crimes he is accused of ("Tabula Rasa").

MLA WORKS CITED PAGE

A Works Cited must be included at the end of the paper. Each source cited in the text must have a corresponding Works Cited entry.

- Begin the Works Cited on a separate page, formatted with one-inch margins and running header that contains a last name and page number, which continues from the last page of the essay. Center the words Works Cited as the title at the top of the page. Do not use italics, bolding, underlining, or quotation marks.
- List entries alphabetically by the author's (or editor's) last name, using last name, first name format. Do not list titles (e.g., Dr.) or degrees (e.g., PhD), but include suffixes such as "Jr." (e.g., Gates, Henry Louis, Jr.).
- Use a hanging indent for each entry more than one line in length. Double space all citations, and do not add extra spaces between entries.
- Capitalize each word in the title, with the exception of conjunctions, prepositions, or articles (such as a, an, the) unless it is the first word of the title or subtitle: *Everything Is Illuminated, The Art of War, For Whom the Bell Tolls.*
- List page numbers efficiently. For example, if referencing a work that appeared on pages 136 through 153, list the page numbers as 136–53.
- Use italics for larger works (books, movies, magazines) and quotation marks for shorter works (articles, songs, essays, poems).

MLA Style

MLA 8: The Works Cited List

Given that new mediums are being introduced constantly and some publication types now include more than one medium or blur the lines between traditional mediums, MLA 8 included a general list to follow for citing sources to ensure that any source can be cited in MLA—even those that have not yet been created. Note that the punctuation that follows each element is the punctuation that should be included in your Works Cited, though your Works Cited entry will always end with a period.

1. Author.
2. Title of Source.
3. Title of Container,
4. Other Contributors,
5. Version,
6. Number,
7. Publisher,
8. Publication date,
9. Page number/s preceded by p. or pp.,
10. Location (If important).

Example 1: Citing the Full Book

Allen, Jason. *A Meditation on Fire: Poems.* Southeast Missouri State University Press, 2016.

Example 2: Citing Part of the Book

Allen, Jason. "Uncle Jeff Jumped Out a Window." *A Meditation on Fire: Poems,* Southeast Missouri State University Press, 2016, p. 25.

Rodriguéz, Jose Antonio. "The Little Rooms." *The Shallow End of Sleep,* Tiá Chucha Press, 2011, pp. 76–77.

Note that because Allen's poem, "Uncle Jeff Jumped Out a Window" is only one page, we use "p. 25" in the Works Cited entry. Since Rodriguéz's poem is two pages, we use "pp. 76–77."

MLA 8 uses the term "container" to indicate the site of a given source, such as the website that houses the article or the journal from which an article came. If a source has multiple containers (e.g., the article came from a journal found in ProQuest), your citation may extend beyond the directions above. Consult the chart below for assistance with sources with more than one container.

1 Author.
2. Title.
3. Title of container,
4. Other contributors (translators or editors),
5. Version (edition),

6. Number (vol. and/or no.),
7. Publisher,
8. Publisher Date,
9. Location,
10. Page Numbers (preceded with p. or pp.).
11. 2nd container's title,
12. Other contributors,
13. Version,
14. Number,
15. Publisher,
16. Date of Publication,
17. Location (if necessary).

Print Sources

Books

One Author
When a book has one author, list the author's name in last name, first name format.

Sedaris, David. *Barrel Fever*. Little, Brown, 1994.

Two or Three Authors
Use the last name, first name format for the first author; then list other author names by first name, last name.

Ward, Geoffrey, Ken Burns, and Kevin Baker. *Baseball: An Illustrated History*. Alfred A. Knopf, Inc., 1996.

Three or More Authors
For more than three authors, you may include each author's name, or you may list only the first author followed by et al., rather than listing the additional authors' names. The et in et al. should not be followed by a period.

Barnes, Sonya, et al. *Image Power: Top Image Experts Share What to Know to Look Your Best*. PowerDynamics Publishing, 2008.

Two or More Works by the Same Author
For more than one work by the same author, list the entries alphabetically by title, and use three hyphens rather than the author's name for each entry after the first:

Bartholomae, David. "Inventing the University." [...]

---. "The Tidy House: Basic Writing in the American Curriculum." [...]

MLA Style

Work by an Unknown Author
Works by an unknown author should be alphabetized by their title.

Beowulf. [...]

Author with an Editor
Begin with the author, then include the editor after the title.

Fielding, Henry. *Tom Jones.* Edited by Sheridan Baker, W. W. Norton & Company, Inc., 1973.

Editor with no Author
Begin with the title of the piece, then provide the editor name.

Che: The Life, Death, and Afterlife of a Revolutionary. Edited by Joseph Hart, Thunder's Mouth Press, 2003.

Author with a Translator
List the entry by author name, then include the translator after the title.

Gide, André. *Lafcadio's Adventures.* Translated by Dorothy Bussy, Vintage Books, 1953.

A Work in an Anthology
Begin with the author name, then the title of the article or chapter in quotation marks. List the anthology title in italics, followed by the editor's name.

Bartholomae, David. "Inventing the University." *When a Writer Can't Write.* Edited by Mike Rose, Guilford, 1985, pp. 134–65.

Encyclopedia/Dictionary Entry
For entries in reference works, cite the entry by the term being referenced. Do not include publisher information or page number.

"Citation." *The Shorter Oxford English Dictionary.* 5th ed., 2002.

Periodicals
List the author of the article first, then include the article title in quotation marks and the periodical title in italics. Follow with the date of publication, and abbreviate all months.

Article in a Magazine
Miller, Jeremy. "The Tyranny of the Test: One Year as a Kaplan Coach in the Public Schools." *Harper's Magazine*, 2 Sept. 2008, pp. 35–46.

Article in a Newspaper
Timson, Judith. "Stop All That Multitasking, Study Suggests." *The Toronto Star*, 7 Aug. 2001, p. E2.

Article in a Scholarly Journal
Provide issue numbers, when available.

Collins, Terence, and Melissa Blum. "Meanness and Failure: Sanctioning Basic Writers." *Journal of Basic Writing*, vol. 19, no. 1, 2000, pp. 13–21.

Personal Interview/Personal Communication
Personal interviews are interviews you conduct yourself. List the interview by the name of the interviewee and include "Personal interview" and the date of the interview.

Smith, Jane. Personal interview. 19 May 2014.

Electronic Sources
Because web sites are often updated and the same information may not be available later, it is a good practice to list your date of access, even though MLA 8 does not require it.

Web Site
List the name of the organization hosting the web site, followed by the name of the site. Use n.d. if no publishing date is given. Include the DOI or Permalink if available, otherwise include the URL (without http://), followed by the date of access.

National Public Radio. *Morning Edition*. NPR, 14 Jan. 2014, www.npr.org/programs/morning-edition. Accessed 26 Apr. 2014.

Web Page
List the author if known, followed by the information required for web sites.

Abdullah, Mardziah Hayati. "The Impact of Electronic Communication on Writing." *EricDigests.org*. ERIC Clearinghouse on Reading, English, and Communication, Dec. 2003, www.ericdigests.org/2004-1/impact.htm. Accessed 13 Oct. 2004.

Online Book
List the entry by author name, title of book in italics, followed by the organization hosting the page.

Austen, Jane. *Pride and Prejudice*. Project Gutenberg, 2013, www.gutenberg.org/files/1342/1342-h/1342-h.htm. Accessed 14 Apr. 2014.

Article in an Online Magazine
Start with the author name, followed by the article name in quotation marks, title of the online magazine in italics, publisher name, publication date, medium, and date of access.

Remnick, David. "Putin and the Exile." *New Yorker*. NewYorker.com, 28 Apr. 2014, www.newyorker.com/magazine/2014/04/28/putin-and-the-exile. Accessed 28 Apr. 2014.

MLA Style

MLA Style

Article in an Online Scholarly Journal
Use the same format as a scholarly journal in print, but include the DOI or permalink and list the date of access.

Soliday, Mary. "From the Margins to the Mainstream: Reconceiving Remediation." *College Composition and Communication*, vol. 47, no. 1, 1996, pp. 85–100, www.jstor.org/stable/358275. Accessed 14 Jan. 2014.

Film
List films by their title in italics, followed by the director's name, then list performer names if relevant. Follow with the distributor and release year.

The Wolf of Wall Street. Directed by Martin Scorsese, performances by Leonardo DiCaprio, Jonah Hill, Matthew McConaughey, Kyle Chandler, and Jon Favreau, Paramount, 2013.

Broadcast Program
Begin with the title of the episode in quotation marks, then the name of the program in italics. Include the network name, call letters of the station and the city, and broadcast date.

"Unsolvable." *Brooklyn Nine-Nine*. Fox, WXMI, Grand Rapids, 19 Mar. 2014.

Recorded Episode
List the entry by episode name in quotation marks, followed by the series name in italics, the distributor name, and the date of distribution.

"Tabula Rasa." *Criminal Minds: Season 3*, written by Jeff Davis, Dan Sworkin, and Jay Beattie, directed by Steve Boyum, Paramount, 2010.

Music or Sound Recording
Begin with the artist name, then put song titles in quotation marks and album names in italics. If relevant, list composer or performer information after the album title. Include the recording company and publication date (or n.d., if date is unknown).

The Beatles. *Revolver*. EMI, 2009.

Beyoncé. "Pray You Catch Me." *Lemonade*, Parkwood Entertainment, 2016, www.beyonce.com/album/lemonade-visual-album/. Accessed 6 Feb. 2017.

Miranda, Lin-Manuel. *The Hamilton Mixtape*, Atlantic Records, 2016.

Yo-Yo Ma. *Yo-Yo Ma Plays Ennio Morricone*, composed by Ennio Morricone, Sony Masterworks, 2010.

Student Style Manual for MLA, Chicago, and APA Documentation

Chicago Style (CMS)

The *Chicago Manual of Style*, or CMS, is a style guide created by the University of Chicago Press in the early twentieth century, to establish formatting rules and bring consistency to their publications. Chicago style is most often used in the social sciences, arts, and humanities disciplines, such as history, art, philosophy, music, theatre, and religious studies. The most recent publication, the 16th edition, was published in 2010.

CMS GUIDELINES FOR FORMATTING PAPERS

- The essay should be typed, double spaced in 12-point font size, in an easy-to-read font (such as Times New Roman) on 8.5-inch by 11-inch paper, with 1-inch margins on all sides.

- Include a title page, with the title centered a third of the way down the page, and the author's name and any other relevant information centered a few lines down from the title.

- Paginate the essay in the top right corner of the page, beginning with the first page of the text (not the title page).

- Change underlining to italics. However, some underlining may need to be preserved, depending on the original material.

- Fix commas and periods relative to quotation marks (commas and periods go inside the quotation marks, not outside: "Chapter 1," rather than "Chapter 1", for example).

- Use em dashes (—) and ellipses (…) where appropriate, and make consistent.

- Replace hyphens (-) with en dashes (–) where appropriate.

- Leave one character space, rather than two spaces, between words and sentences and after colons.

- Use double spacing for text, except in block quotations. Use single spacing for footnotes and bibliography/reference lists, with a line to separate entries.

- The bibliography should begin on a new page, separate from the essay.

Chicago Style (CMS)

CMS General In-Text Citation and Footnote Rules

CMS In-Text Citations and Footnotes

Note Numbers

Note reference numbers in text are superscripted. In the notes themselves, they are full size and followed by a period.

Sedaris recalls, "We rode round and round the block on our pony, who groaned beneath the collective weight of our rich and overwhelming capacity for love and understanding."[1]

   1. David Sedaris, *Barrel Fever* (New York: Little, Brown, 1994), 9–10.

Notes should be numbered consecutively, beginning with 1, throughout the essay. A note number should generally be placed at the end of a sentence, a clause, or a quotation. The number follows any punctuation mark except for the dash, which it precedes.

Many students argue that they work better when multitasking[5]—but research suggests this may not be the case.

Bibliographic citations are provided in footnotes (which appear at the bottom of a page), supplemented by a bibliography at the end of the work. Footnotes are numbered (but not superscripted) and correspond to superscripted note reference numbers in the text.

Full Footnote Citation

   1. David Sedaris, *Barrel Fever* (New York: Little, Brown, 1994), 36–37.

Short Footnote Citation

   1. Sedaris, *Barrel Fever*, 36–37.

Entry in a Bibliography

   Sedaris, David. *Barrel Fever*. New York: Little, Brown. 1994.

If the same source is used consecutively in the text, the source should be formatted as usual for the first entry, and "Ibid." and the relevant page number, if different than the first note, should be used for each subsequent entry, until a different source is used within the text.

   1. David Sedaris, *Barrel Fever* (New York: Little, Brown, 1994), 36.

   2. Ibid.

   3. Ibid., 37.

   4. David Bartholomae, "Inventing the University," in *When a Writer Can't Write*, ed. Mike Rose (New York: Guilford, 1985), 146.

Shortened Citations

Because the complete citation information is available in the corresponding bibliography, using the short footnote citation is acceptable in Chicago style.

The short form of a citation should include enough information to lead readers to the appropriate entry in the bibliography. The short form consists of the last name of the author, the main title of the work cited (usually shortened if more than four words), and the page number indicating where the information is located.

> 1. David Bartholomae, "Inventing the University," in *When a Writer Can't Write*, ed. Mike Rose (New York: Guilford, 1985), 146.

> 2. Bartholomae, "Inventing the University," 146.

Using In-Text Sources

It is important to provide a lead-in to source quotations, summaries, or paraphrases in the text, especially the first time the source is used. Lead-ins introduce the sources to the audience and provide a smooth transition from the author's writing to quotes, summaries, and paraphrases within the text.

Block Quotations

For quotations longer than four lines in length, add an extra line space and indent 1/2 inch from the left margin. Place the whole quote, single spaced, within the new margin. Do not use quotation marks. The note number should come after the end punctuation.

As a builder, Lubbers was tasked to determine the most effective method for ensuring the safety and integrity of structures in a variety of climates. Lubbers's study found the following:

> The prevailing wind being forecast for January 2 will be from the southwest, and will reach speeds of up to 50 miles per hour. This wind has the potential to cause significant damage to the current construction. The building should be braced heavily to avoid collapse.[3]

Because the formatting for footnotes is consistent regardless of the medium being cited, not all areas that follow will include in-text citation examples.

Books

One Author

In-Text Citation

Sedaris recalls, "We rode round and round the block on our pony, who groaned beneath the collective weight of our rich and overwhelming capacity for love and understanding."[1]

Short Footnote Citation

> 1. Sedaris, *Barrel Fever*, 9–10.

Two to Three Authors

In-Text Citation

Collins and Blum outline the way socioeconomics and politics outside the university also play a role in instigating the division between "basic" and "normal" writers.[3]

Short Footnote Citation

    3. Collins and Blum, "Meanness and Failure," 14.

More than Three Authors

In-Text Citation

Cincotta et al. assert that the launch of Sputnik expanded the competitive arena between the U.S. and the Soviet Union.[2]

Short Footnote Citation

    2. Howard Cincotta et al., *An Outline of American History* (Washington D.C.: United States Information Agency, 1994).

Unknown Author

In-Text Citation

A study determined that subjects lose time when switching from task to task.[4]

Short Footnote Citation

    4. "Is Multitasking," 3.

Editor as Author

This type of source includes information written by the editor of an anthology, as in a foreword, introduction, afterword, or editor's notes. In these cases, the editor should be treated as the author of the source being used.

In-Text Citation

Historian Joseph Hart asserts, "Ernesto Che Guevara's death at the hands of Bolivian troops last October enhanced a legend that began when he was Fidel Castro's right-hand man in Cuba."[5]

Short Footnote Citation

    5. Hart, *Che*, 3.

Bibliography Entry

Hart, Joseph, ed. *Che: The Life, Death, and Afterlife of a Revolutionary.* New York: Thunder's Mouth Press, 2003.

Work in an Anthology

Please note that in these cases, the author of the work being quoted will be the primary reference in the text, the footnote, and the bibliography; the anthology editor(s) will also be included in the bibliography entry. A bibliography entry is included here as an example.

In-Text Citation

According to David Bartholomae, students who were less successful at this "invention" were considered basic writers; those who were more successful were not.[6]

Long Footnote Citation

     6. David Bartholomae, "Inventing the University," in *When a Writer Can't Write*, ed. Mike Rose (New York: Guilford, 1985), 134–65.

Short Footnote Citation

     6. Bartholomae, "Inventing the University," 146–47.

Bibliography Entry

Bartholomae, David. "Inventing the University." In *When a Writer Can't Write*, edited by Mike Rose, 134–65. New York: Guilford, 1985.

Periodicals

Article in a Journal

In-Text Citation

Teacher-researchers Terence Collins and Melissa Blum pointed to the ways that socioeconomics and politics outside of the university also played a role in instigating the division between "basic" and "normal" writers.[7]

Short Footnote Citation

     7. Collins and Blum, "Meanness and Failure," 14.

Article in a Magazine

Short Footnote Citation

     8. Miller, "The Tyranny of the Test," 39.

Article in a Newspaper

Note that Chicago style does not require newspaper articles to be included in the bibliography, as long as they have been included in the text and footnotes. In these cases, however, the long footnote citation should be used.

Long Footnote Citation

     9. Eric Pianin, "Use of Arsenic in Wood Products to End," *Washington Post*, February 13, 2002, final edition.

Entry in an Encyclopedia/Dictionary

Though cited in the footnotes, well-known reference materials are typically not cited in the bibliography, and the publication information is often omitted. If the publication is not the first edition, the edition number must be included.

Footnote Citation

> 10. *The Shorter Oxford English Dictionary*, 5th ed., s.v. "citation."

Personal Interview/Personal Communication

Personal interviews are included as a note only; they do not need to be included in the bibliography.

> 11. Danny Williams, e-mail message to author, June 15, 2017.

Electronic Sources

Article from an Online Periodical

Follow the same guidelines as printed articles and include the URL or, if available, the digital object identifier (DOI).

Scholarly Journal

> 12. Adler-Kassner and Harrington, "Responsibility and Composition's Future," 77. http://www.jstor.org/discover/10.2307/27917885?uid=3739728&uid=2129&uid=2&uid=70&uid=4&uid=3739256&sid=21104117601803.

Article in a Popular Magazine

> 13. Remnick, "Putin and the Exile." http://www.newyorker.com/talk/comment/2014/04/28/140428taco_talk_remnick.

Online Newspaper Article

Remember that Chicago style does not require newspaper articles to be included in the bibliography. Additionally, a URL need not be included for online newspaper sources; however, the long footnote citation must be used.

Long Footnote Citation

> 14. Felicia R. Lee, "Trying to Bring Baldwin's Complex Voice Back," *The New York Times*, April 24, 2014.

Online Encyclopedia/Dictionary Entry

> 15. *Merriam-Webster Online*, s.v. "citation," accessed April 26, 2014, http://www.merriam-webster.com/dictionary/citation.

Film

> 16. *Big Fish*, directed by Tim Burton. (2003; Culver City, CA: Sony Home Pictures Entertainment, 2004), DVD.

Single Episode of a Television Series

17. Jeff Davis, Dan Sworkin, and Jay Beattie, "Tabula Rasa," *Criminal Minds*, season 3, episode 19, directed by Steve Boyum, aired May 14, 2008. (Los Angeles, CA: Paramount, 2010), DVD.

Music or Sound Recording

Album

18. The Beatles, *Revolver*, EMI, 2009, CD.

Song

19. Miranda Lambert, vocal performance of "Heart Like Mine," by Travis Howard, Miranda Lambert, and Ashley Monroe, recorded 2009, on *Revolution*, Columbia Nashville, CD.

CMS BIBLIOGRAPHY PAGE

A bibliography must be included at the end of the essay when using footnotes. All sources to be included—books, articles, web sites—are arranged alphabetically by the last names of the authors (or, if no author or editor is given, alphabetically by the title or other identifying word or phrase).

- Entries should have a hanging indent—all lines after the first line of each entry should be indented one-half inch from the left margin.
- Bibliography entries should be alphabetized by the last name of the first author of each work, and the author should be listed in last name, first name format.
- List entries for multiple articles by the same author in chronological order, from earliest to most recent.
- Include the complete title, maintaining the capitalization and punctuation used in the original title.
- Italicize titles of longer works, such as books and journals, and put quotes around the titles of shorter works, such as journal articles or essays in edited collections. Do not italicize or underline them.

Formatting Bibliography Entries

Books

Information to Include

- Full name(s) of author(s) or editor(s)
- Complete title (including subtitle) of book and edition, if not the first
- Publication information (city, publisher, date)
- Page reference for a chapter, essay, or other section of a book. Complete book sources do not include page numbers in the bibliography.
- DOI or URL for online books

One Author

Sedaris, David. *Barrel Fever*. New York: Little, Brown, 1994.

Two Works by the Same Author

To list two or more works by the same author in the bibliography, use three em-dashes followed by a period in place of the author name for each entry after the first.

Sedaris, David. *Barrel Fever*. New York: Little, Brown, 1994.

———. *Me Talk Pretty One Day*. New York: Little, Brown, 2000.

Two to Three Authors

Ward, Geoffrey, Ken Burns, and Kevin Baker. *Baseball: An Illustrated History*. New York: Alfred A. Knopf, Inc., 1996.

More than Three Authors

Barnes, Sonya et al. *Image Power: Top Image Experts Share What to Know to Look Your Best*. San Francisco: PowerDynamics Publishing, 2008.

Unknown Author

Beowulf. New York: Farrar, Straus and Giroux, 2000.

Author with an Editor

Fielding, Henry. *Tom Jones*, edited by Sheridan Baker. New York: W.W. Norton & Company, Inc., 1994.

Editor with no Author

Hart, Joseph, ed. *Che: The Life, Death, and Afterlife of a Revolutionary*. New York: Thunder's Mouth Press, 2003.

Author with a Translator

Gide, André. *Lafcadio's Adventures*. Translated by Dorothy Bussy. New York: Vintage Books, 1953.

Work in an Anthology

Bartholomae, David. "Inventing the University." In *When a Writer Can't Write*, edited by Mike Rose, 134–65. New York: Guilford, 1985.

Periodicals

Information to Include
- Full name(s) of author(s)
- Complete title (including subtitle) of article
- Title of periodical
- Volume number, issue number, date
- Page reference. Please note that if a page number is not available, a chapter or paragraph number or section header may be included.
- DOI or URL for online periodicals

Article in a Magazine
Miller, Jeremy. "The Tyranny of the Test: One Year as a Kaplan Coach in the Public Schools." *Harper's Magazine* September 2008.

Article in Journal Paginated by Issue
Because journals are paginated by issue, begin with page one for each issue and include the issue number in the citation.

Collins, Terence and Melissa Blum. "Meanness and Failure: Sanctioning Basic Writers." *Journal of Basic Writing* 19, no. 1 (2000): 13–21.

Article in Journal Paginated by Volume
Journals paginated by volume begin with page one in issue one, and page numbers continue in issue two where issue one left off. Therefore, it is not necessary to include an issue number.

Sledd, Andrew. "Readin' not Riotin': The Politics of Literacy." *College English* 50 (1998): 495–508.

Electronic Sources
Include all available relevant publication information, including the URL or, if available, the DOI.

Web Site
National Public Radio. *Morning Edition.* Accessed January 14, 2014. http://www.npr.org/programs/morning-edition.

Web Page
Abdullah, Mardziah Hayati. "The Impact of Electronic Communication on Writing." *ERIC Clearinghouse on Reading, English, and Communication.* http://www.ericdigests.org/2004-1/impact.htm.

Online Book

Austen, Jane. *Pride and Prejudice*. London, 1813. http://www.gutenberg. org/catalog/world/readfile?fk_files=3381939.

Article from an Online Periodical

Popular Magazine

Remnick, David. "Putin and the Exile." *New Yorker*, April 28, 2014, accessed April 28, 2014. http://www.newyorker.com/talk/comment/2014/04/ 28/140428taco_talk_remnick.

Scholarly Journal

Soliday, Mary. "From the Margins to the Mainstream: Reconceiving Remediation." *College Composition and Communication* 47, no. 1 (1996): 85–100. Accessed January 14, 2014. http://www.jstor.org/ stable/358275.

Video/Film

McGregor, Ewan, Albert Finney, Jessica Lange, Billy Crudup, and Marion Cotillard. *Big Fish*. DVD. Directed by Tim Burton. Culver City: Sony Home Pictures Entertainment, 2003.

Broadcast Program

Begin with the writer(s), followed by the name of the program in italics. Also include the director's name, broadcast date, distribution city and company, and publication medium (e.g., Television, Radio).

Door, Daniel, and Michael Schur. *Brooklyn Nine-Nine*. Directed by Ken Whittingham. 2014. Los Angeles: NBCUniversal Television Distribution.

Television Episode

Begin with the writer(s), followed by the name of episode in quotation marks and the program title in italics. Also include the season number, episode number, director's name, original broadcast date, distribution city and company, release date, and publication medium (e.g., Television, Radio).

Davis, Jeff, Dan Sworkin, and Jay Beattie, "Tabula Rasa." *Criminal Minds*, season 3, episode 19, directed by Steve Boyum, aired May 14, 2008. (Los Angeles: Paramount, 2010), DVD.

Sound Recording

List artist, title of album in italics, city and name of distribution company, medium, and date of original release.

Miranda, Lin-Manuel. *The Hamilton Mixtape*. New York: Atlantic Records, CD. Recorded 2016.

Student Style Manual for MLA, Chicago, and APA Documentation

APA Style

The *Publication Manual of the American Psychological Association*, or APA, is a style guide created by the American Psychological Association to establish formatting rules and bring consistency to their publications. Academic disciplines such as psychology, sociology, economics, business, and nursing, typically use APA style. The most recent publication, the 6th edition, was published in 2009 and updated in 2016.

APA Guidelines for Formatting Papers

- Start with a header that says "Running head:" followed immediately by a shortened version of the paper title in all caps, aligned to the left in the upper left corner of the page. On the same line, but aligned to the right of the page, will be "1" to indicate that the title page is your first page.

- Write your title again, this time centered in the upper half of the page and in title case, with the author's name centered below and then the author's institutional affiliation centered below that. In title case, upper-case letters begin each word with the exception of articles and prepositions.

- All of the text on the title page should be double spaced in a 12-point, easy-to-read font (such as Times New Roman).

- The essay should be typed, double spaced in 12-point, easy-to-read font (such as Times New Roman) on 8.5-inch by 11-inch paper, with 1-inch margins on all sides.

- Beginning with the second page, include the abbreviated title of your paper (50 characters max.) in all capital letters in a header aligned to the left. On the same line, but aligned right, include the page number.

- Change underlining to italics. However, some underlining may need to be preserved, depending on the original material.

APA Style

Running head: ABBREVIATED TITLE OF PAPER   1

Title of Paper

Your Name

Your College or University

Sample APA Title Page

- If your instructor requires you to include an abstract, which is commonly included in scholarly articles, the abstract will be on page 2 and will include the abbreviated title of your paper in all capital letters in a header aligned to the left. On the same line, but aligned right, include the page number. If you are not required to include an abstract, begin your paper on the second page.

- Fix commas and periods relative to quotation marks (commas and periods go inside the quotation marks, not outside: "Chapter 1," rather than "Chapter 1", for example).

- Use em dashes (—) and ellipses (...) where appropriate, and be consistent.

- Replace hyphens (-) with en dashes (–) where appropriate.

- The second printing of the 6th edition of the APA style guide recommends, but does not require, using two spaces after the end punctuation of a sentence, for ease of readability.

- The reference page should begin on a new page, separate from the essay.

APA General In-Text Citation Rules

- It is important to provide a lead-in to source quotations or paraphrases in the text, especially the first time the source is used. Lead-ins introduce the sources to the audience and provide a smooth transition to quotes and paraphrases within the text.

- While it is important to include page numbers when directly quoting from a source, you do not have to provide the page number when paraphrasing or summarizing an idea from a source. However, for pedagogical reasons, some professors will prefer that you include page numbers so it is always smart to ask in advance.

- Though authors writing in APA do not commonly reference the titles of works in their texts, if you do reference the title of a source in text:

  - Capitalize all words that are four letters long or more within the title of a source: *Pride and Prejudice*. Short words that are verbs, nouns, pronouns, adjectives, and adverbs are exceptions to this rule: *Everything Is Illuminated*, *Brave New World*.

  - Italicize the titles of longer works such as books, movies, anthologies, television series, or albums: *American Idol*; *Anchorman*. Put quotation marks around the titles of shorter works within the text, such as journal articles, essays in anthologies, and song titles: "Red"; "Inventing the University."

  - Capitalize both words in a hyphenated compound word: *The Tell-Tale Heart*. Also capitalize the first word after a colon or dash: *The World Is Flat: A Brief History of the Twenty-First Century*.

APA Style

A Work by a Single Author

If quoting directly from a work, include the author, year of publication, and the page number (preceded by "p." for a single page or "pp." for multiple pages). When not directly quoting, exclude page numbers from the citation.

Sedaris (1994) recalls, "We rode round and round the block on our pony, who groaned beneath the collective weight of our rich and overwhelming capacity for love and understanding" (pp. 9–10).

"We rode round and round the block on our pony, who groaned beneath the collective weight of our rich and overwhelming capacity for love and understanding" (Sedaris, 1994, pp. 9–10).

Sedaris (1994) recalls circling his neighborhood atop his pony.

Block Quotations

Start quotations longer than 40 words on a new line, indented 1/2 inch from the left margin. Place the whole quote, double spaced, on the new margin. The parenthetical citation follows the end punctuation. Do not use quotation marks.

As a builder, Lubbers was tasked to determine the most effective method for ensuring the safety and integrity of structures in a variety of climates. Lubbers's (2013) study found the following:

> The prevailing wind being forecast for January 2 will be from the south-west, and will reach speeds of up to 50 miles per hour. This wind has the potential to cause significant damage to the current construction. The building should be braced heavily to avoid collapse. (p. 202)

Print Sources

Two Authors

List both authors whenever the work is cited. In the signal phrase, "and" should be used between the authors' names, while an ampersand (&) should be used in the parentheses.

Research by Collins and Blum (2000) outlines the way socioeconomics and politics outside the university also play a role in instigating the division between "basic" and "normal" writers (p. 14).

Researcher scholars outline the way socioeconomics and politics outside the university also play a role in instigating the division between "basic" and "normal" writers (Collins & Blum, 2000, p. 14).

Three to Five Authors

List all the authors by last name the first time the source is cited. In later citations, use the first author's last name followed by "et al." The et in et al. should not be followed by a period.

Ward, Burns, and Baker (1996) note, "The game varied from state to state, town to town, but town ball was the most popular" (p. 4).

(Ward et al., 1996, p. 4)

Six or More Authors

Use the first author's last name, followed by et al. You do not have to provide the page number when paraphrasing or summarizing from a source, but some professors will prefer that you do so; it is always smart to ask in advance.

Cincotta et al. (1994) assert that the launch of Sputnik expanded the competitive arena between the U.S. and the Soviet Union.

Unknown Author

If the author of a source is unknown, cite using the title in the lead-in, or include an abbreviated version of the title in the parenthetical citation.

A similar study determined that subjects lose time when switching from task to task ("Is Multitasking," 2001).

Authors with the Same Last Name

Include first initials with the last names to distinguish between the authors.

(R. Jones, 2012; A. Jones, 2003)

Anthology

According to David Bartholomae (1985), students who were less successful at this "invention" were considered basic writers; those who were more successful were not (p. 136).

Encyclopedia/Dictionary Entry

A citation is a "quotation from or reference to a book, paper, or author" (Citation, 2002).

APA Style

Indirect Sources

It may be necessary to use a work that has been cited in another source. Though it may seem strange, include the citations embedded within the original material you are quoting. You need not include the original work in your reference page unless you draw from the work elsewhere in your paper.

Young (2010) anticipates Fish's response, stating: "To this objection, Victor Villanueva, a Puerto Rican scholar of American studies, as well as language and literacy, point to 'writers of color who have been using the blended form [...] from the get-go' (351)" (p. 116).

Personal Interview/ Personal Communication

Personal communications are not included in the reference list. Cite the communicator's name, the phrase "personal communication," and the date of the communication parenthetically in your main text only.

Example

Danny Williams states that he and his colleagues experience tension when discussing personal issues (personal communication, June 14, 2017).

Electronic Sources

Web Sources

When possible, cite a web document the same as any other document.

Bianchi (2007) suggests [...]

If no author or date is given, cite using the title in the lead-in, or include an abbreviated version of the title in the parenthetical citation, and use the abbreviation "n.d." ("no date").

A similar study determined that subjects lost more time when switching from a familiar task to an unfamiliar task ("Is Multitasking," n.d.).

If you are directly quoting from the source and no page number is available for material you are directly quoting, include information that will help readers find the material being cited. If paragraphs are numbered, use "para." and follow with the paragraph number.

(Hubbard, 2014, para. 3).

Video/Film

Big Fish (2003), directed by Tim Burton, details the extraordinary life of Edward Bloom.

APA Reference Page

The reference list, including all sources cited in the text, should appear on a separate page at the end of the text. The reference page should include the title "References" centered at the top of the page, with no bolding, underlining, italicizing, or quotation marks. All text in the reference section should be double spaced, with no additional spaces between entries.

- Entries should have a hanging indent—all lines after the first line of each entry should be indented one-half inch from the left margin.
- Reference list entries should be alphabetized by the last name of the first author of each work.
- For multiple articles by the same author, or authors listed in the same order, list the entries in chronological order, from earliest to most recent. In instances in which the same author has multiple works from the same year, list them in order from earliest to most recent with letters following the year (2017a, 2017b, and so on).
- Include the complete journal title in italics, maintaining the capitalization and punctuation used in the original. Include the volume and issue numbers (if applicable).
- When referring to books, chapters, articles, or web pages, capitalize only the first letter of the first word of a title and subtitle, the first word after a colon or a dash in the title, and proper nouns. Do not capitalize the first letter of the second word in a hyphenated compound word.
- Italicize titles of longer works (books, films); do not italicize, underline, or put quotes around the titles of shorter works (articles, songs).

Single Author
Use the last name, initials format. Note that the journal below is published annually, which means it has a volume number, but not an issue number.

Young, V. (2010). Should Writers Use They Own English? *Iowa Journal of Cultural Studies, 12*, 110–117.

Two Authors
List using the last name, initials format and use the ampersand (&) instead of "and."

Collins, T., & Blum, M. (2000). Meanness and failure: Sanctioning basic writers. *Journal of Basic Writing, 19*(1), 13–21.

Three to Seven Authors
Use the last name, initials format, separate authors' names using commas, and precede the final author's name with an ampersand.

Rubenstein, J., Meyer, D., & Evans, J. (2001). Executive control of cognitive processes in task switching. *Journal of Experimental Psychology: Human Perception and Performance, 27*(4), 763–797.

More Than Seven Authors

Follow the same rules as a source with three to seven authors, but after the sixth author's name, use an ellipses rather than listing authors' names. Then list the final author's name. In other words, there should not be more than seven names listed in the citation.

Barnes, S., Buchanan, W., Chenn, H., Elrick, H., Graham, J. A., King, D....
    Law, K. (2008). Web site usability for the blind and low-vision user. In
    Image power: Top image experts share what to know to look your best.
    San Francisco, CA: PowerDynamics Publishing.

Two or More Works by the Same Author

Use the last name, initials format for all entries and list the entries by the year, earliest first.

Child, L. (2007).

Child, L. (2010).

Unknown Author

When a source does not include an author's name, use the source's title (abbreviated, if the title is long) rather than an author's name.

Beowulf. (2000). New York, NY: Farrar, Straus and Giroux.

Books

For the publication location information, include the city and the two-letter state abbreviation (New York, NY).

Basic Format for Books

Sedaris, D. (1994). *Barrel fever.* New York, NY: Little, Brown.

Author with an Editor

Fielding, H. (1973). *Tom Jones.* S. Baker (Ed.). New York, NY: W. W. Norton
    & Company, Inc.

Editor as Author

Hart, J. (Ed.). (2003). *Che: The life, death, and afterlife of a revolutionary.*
    New York, NY: Thunder's Mouth Press.

Author with a Translator

Gide, A. (1953). *Lafcadio's adventures.* (D. Bussy, Trans.). New York, NY:
    Vintage Books. (Original work published 1914).

Work in an Anthology

Bartholomae, D. (1985). Inventing the university. In M. Rose (Ed.), *When a*
    writer can't write (pp. 134–165). New York, NY: Guilford.

Encyclopedia/Dictionary Entry

Citation. (2002). In *The shorter Oxford English dictionary* (5th ed.). Oxford, UK: Oxford University Press.

Periodicals

Authors are listed in last name, initial format, followed by the publication year in parentheses. The title of the article is in sentence case (only the first word and proper nouns are capitalized). The title of the periodical is in title case and is followed by the volume number, both of which are in italics.

Article in a Magazine

Miller, J. (2008, September 2). The tyranny of the test: One year as a Kaplan coach in the public schools. *Harper's Magazine*, 35–46.

Article in a Newspaper

Precede page numbers with p. (for a single page) or pp. (for more than one page).

Timson, J. (2001, August 7). Stop all that multitasking, study suggests. *The Toronto Star*, p. E2.

Article in Journal Paginated by Issue

Because journals paginated by issue begin with page one for each issue, the issue number is included in the citation. The parentheses and issue number are not italicized or underlined.

Collins. T. & Blum, M. (2000). Meanness and failure: Sanctioning basic writers. *Journal of Basic Writing, 19*(1), 13–21.

Article in Journal Paginated by Volume

Journals paginated by volume begin with page one in issue one, and page numbers continue in issue two where issue one left off. Therefore, it is not necessary to include an issue number.

Sledd, A. (1998). Readin' not riotin': The politics of literacy. *College English, 50*, 495–508.

Electronic Sources

Follow the same guidelines as printed articles, and include all available relevant information. Because web sites are often updated and the same information may not be available later, the DOI should be used rather than the URL whenever possible.

Web Site

National Public Radio. (2014, January). *Morning edition.* Retrieved from NPR web site http://www.npr.org/programs/morning-edition/

APA Style

Web Page

Abdullah, M. H. (2004, October). The impact of electronic communication on writing. *ERIC Clearinghouse on Reading, English, and Communication.* Retrieved from http://www.ericdigests.org/2004-1/impact.htm

Online Book

Austen, J. (1813). *Pride and prejudice.* Retrieved from http://www.gutenberg.org/catalog/world/readfile?fk_files=3381939

Article from an Online Magazine

Remnick, D. (2014, April 28). Putin and the exile. *New Yorker.* Retrieved from http://www.newyorker.com/talk/comment/2014/04/28/140428taco_talk_remnick

Article from an Online Periodical

Soliday, M. (1996). From the margins to the mainstream: Reconceiving remediation. *College Composition and Communication, 47*(1). Retrieved from http://www.jstor.org/stable/358275

Video/Film

Cohen, B., Zanuck, R. & Jinks, D. (Producers), & Burton, T. (Director). (2003). *Big fish* [Motion picture]. USA: Sony Home Pictures Entertainment.

Broadcast Program

Goor, D. & Schur, M. (Writers), & Whittingham, K. (Director). (2014, March 19). Unsolvable. *Brooklyn nine-nine.* [Television series]. In D. Goor & M. Schur (Producers). Los Angeles, CA: NBCUniversal Television Distribution.

Television Episode

Davis, J., Sworkin, D., & Beattie, J. (Writers), & Boyum, S. (Director). (2008). Tabula rasa [Television series episode]. In E.A. Bernero (Producer), *Criminal minds.* Los Angeles, CA: Paramount.

Music or Sound Recording

Miranda, L. (2016). *Hamilton Mixtape* [CD]. New York, NY: Atlantic Records.

Student Style Manual for MLA, Chicago, and APA Documentation

Citation Chart

	In-Text Citations
	Print Sources
	Author Named in a Signal Phrase
MLA	Sedaris recalls, "We rode round and round the block on our pony, who groaned beneath the collective weight of our rich and overwhelming capacity for love and understanding" (9–10).
CMS	Sedaris recalls, "We rode round and round the block on our pony, who groaned beneath the collective weight of our rich and overwhelming capacity for love and understanding."[1] 1. David Sedaris, *Barrel Fever* (New York: Little, Brown, 1994), 9–10.
APA	Sedaris (1994) recalls, "We rode round and round the block on our pony, who groaned beneath the collective weight of our rich and overwhelming capacity for love and understanding" (pp. 9–10).
	Author Not Named in a Signal Phrase
MLA	He states, "We rode round and round the block on our pony, who groaned beneath the collective weight of our rich and overwhelming capacity for love and understanding" (Sedaris 9–10).
CMS	He states, "We rode round and round the block on our pony, who groaned beneath the collective weight of our rich and overwhelming capacity for love and understanding."[1] 1. David Sedaris, *Barrel Fever* (New York: Little, Brown, 1994), 9–10.
APA	He states, "We rode round and round the block on our pony, who groaned beneath the collective weight of our rich and overwhelming capacity for love and understanding" (Sedaris, 1994, pp. 9–10).

Citation Chart

	In-Text Citations
	Two or Three Authors
MLA	Collins and Blum outline the way socioeconomics and politics outside the university also play a role in instigating the division between "basic" and "normal" writers (14).
	The authors outline the way socioeconomics and politics outside the university also play a role in instigating the division between "basic" and "normal" writers (Collins and Blum 14).
CMS	Collins and Blum outline the way socioeconomics and politics outside the university also play a role in instigating the division between "basic" and "normal" writers.[3]
	3. Collins and Blum, "Meanness and Failure," 14.
APA	Research by Collins and Blum (2000) outlines the way socioeconomics and politics outside the university also play a role in instigating the division between "basic" and "normal" writers (p. 14).
	More Than Three Authors
MLA	Cincotta et al. assert that the launch of Sputnik expanded the competitive arena between the U.S. and the Soviet Union (68).
	Historians assert that the launch of Sputnik expanded the competitive arena between the U.S. and the Soviet Union (Cincotta et al. 68).
	Cincotta, Brown, Burant, Green, Holden, and Marshall assert that the launch of Sputnik expanded the competitive arena between the U.S. and the Soviet Union (68).
CMS	Cincotta et al. assert that the launch of Sputnik expanded the competitive arena between the U.S. and the Soviet Union.[2]
	2. Howard Cincotta et al., *An Outline of American History* (Washington D.C.: United States Information Agency, 1994).
APA	For the first use in text, list all author names:
	Cincotta, Brown, Burant, Green, Holden, and Marshall (1994) [...]
	For subsequent entries, use et al.:
	Cincotta et al. (1994) assert that the launch of Sputnik expanded the competitive arena between the U.S. and the Soviet Union.
	Unknown Author
MLA	A study determined that subjects lose time when switching from task to task ("Is Multitasking" 3).
CMS	A study determined that subjects lose time when switching from task to task.[4]
	Short citation:
	4. "Is Multitasking," 3.
APA	A similar study determined that subjects lose time when switching from task to task ("Is Multitasking," 2001, p. 3).

In-Text Citations	
Work in an Anthology	
MLA	According to David Bartholomae, students who were less successful at this "invention" were considered basic writers; those who were more successful were not (136).
CMS	According to David Bartholomae, students who were less successful at this "invention" were considered basic writers; those who were more successful were not.[6] 6. David Bartholomae, "Inventing the University," in *When a Writer Can't Write*, ed. Mike Rose (New York: Guilford, 1985). 134–65.
APA	According to David Bartholomae (1985), students who were less successful at this "invention" were considered basic writers; those who were more successful were not (p. 136).
Encyclopedia/Dictionary	
MLA	A citation is a "quotation from or reference to a book, paper, or author" ("Citation").
CMS	A citation is a "quotation from or reference to a book, paper, or author."[10] **Use footnote only; does not appear in bibliography.** 10. *The Shorter Oxford English Dictionary*, 5th ed., s.v. "citation."
APA	A citation is a "quotation from or reference to a book, paper, or author" (Citation, 2002).
Electronic Sources	
Web Sources	
MLA	For electronic sources, include the first item (author name, title, etc.) in the Works Cited entry that corresponds to the citation. Do not include URLs in the text unless absolutely necessary; if included, make the URL as brief as possible, such as npr.org rather than http://www.npr.org.
CMS	When possible, follow the same guidelines for printed materials. Include all available information, including the URL or, if available, the digital object identifier (DOI), and use the long footnote citation format.
APA	When possible, cite a web document the same as any other document. If no author or date is given, cite using the title in the lead-in, or include an abbreviated version of the title in the parenthetical citation, and use the abbreviation "n.d." ("no date"). If no page number is available and you are quoting from the source, include information that will help readers find the material being cited. If paragraphs are numbered, use "para." and follow with the paragraph number.

Citation Chart

In-Text Citations	
Film	
MLA	*Big Fish*, directed by Tim Burton, details the extraordinary life of Edward Bloom (2003).
CMS	*Big Fish*, directed by Tim Burton, details the extraordinary life of Edward Bloom.[15] 15. *Big Fish*, directed by Tim Burton (2003; Culver City, CA: Sony Home Pictures Entertainment, 2004), DVD.
APA	*Big Fish* (2003), directed by Tim Burton, details the extraordinary life of Edward Bloom.

End-of-Text Citations		
Books		
General Book Format		
MLA Works Cited	Sedaris, David. *Barrel Fever*. Little, Brown, 1994.	
CMS Bibliography	Sedaris, David. *Barrel Fever*. New York: Little, Brown, 1994.	
APA References	Sedaris, D. (1994). *Barrel fever*. New York, NY: Little, Brown.	
Two or Three Authors		
MLA	Ward, Geoffrey, Ken Burns, and Kevin Baker. *Baseball: An Illustrated History*. Alfred A. Knopf, Inc. 1996.	
CMS	Ward, Geoffrey, Ken Burns, and Kevin Baker. *Baseball: An Illustrated History*. New York: Alfred A. Knopf, Inc., 1996.	
APA	Ward, G., Burns, K., & Baker, K. (1996). *Baseball: An illustrated history*. New York: Alfred A Knopf, Inc.	
More Than Three Authors		
MLA	Barnes, Sonya, et al. [...]	
CMS	Barnes, Sonya et al. [...]	
APA	Three to seven authors: Rubenstein, J., Meyer, D., & Evans, J. (2001). [...] More than seven authors: Barnes, S., Buchanan, W., Chenn, H., Elrick, H., Graham, J. A., King, D....Law, K. (2008). [...]	
Unknown Author		
MLA	*Beowulf*. Farrar, Straus and Giroux, 2000.	
CMS	*Beowulf*. New York: Farrar, Straus and Giroux, 2000.	
APA	*Beowulf*. (2000). New York, NY: Farrar, Straus and Giroux.	
Author with an Editor		
MLA	Fielding, Henry. *Tom Jones*. Edited by Sheridan Baker, [...]	
CMS	Fielding, Henry. *Tom Jones*, edited by Sheridan Baker. [...]	
APA	Fielding, H. (1973). *Tom Jones*. S. Baker (Ed.). [...]	

Citation Chart

End-of-Text Citations	
Editor with no Author	
MLA	*Impossibly Funky: A* Cashiers du Cinemart *Collection.* Edited by M. White, [...]
CMS	White, M., ed. [...]
APA	White, M. (Ed.). (2010). *Impossibly funky: A* Cashiers du Cinemart *collection.* [...]
Author with a Translator	
MLA	Gide, André. *Lafcadio's Adventures.* Translated by Dorothy Bussy, [...]
CMS	Gide, André. *Lafcadio's Adventures.* Translated by Dorothy Bussy. [...]
APA	Gide, A. (1953). *Lafcadio's adventures.* (D. Bussy, Trans.). [...]
Work in an Anthology	
MLA	Bartholomae, David. "Inventing the University." *When a Writer Can't Write,* edited by Mike Rose, Guilford, 1985, pp. 134–65.
CMS	Bartholomae, David. "Inventing the University." In *When a Writer Can't Write,* edited by Mike Rose, 134–65. New York: Guilford, 1985.
APA	Bartholomae, D. (1985). Inventing the university. In M. Rose (Ed.), *When a writer can't write* (pp. 134–165). New York: Guilford.
Encyclopedia/Dictionary Entry	
MLA	"Citation." *The Shorter Oxford English Dictionary.* 5th ed., 2002.
CMS	**In footnotes only.**
APA	Citation. (2002). In *The shorter Oxford English dictionary.* (5th ed.). [...]
Articles in Periodicals	
Magazine	
MLA	Miller, Jeremy. "The Tyranny of the Test: One Year as a Kaplan Coach in the Public Schools." *Harper's Magazine,* 2 Sept. 2008, pp. 35–46.
CMS	Miller, Jeremy. "The Tyranny of the Test: One Year as a Kaplan Coach in the Public Schools." *Harper's Magazine* September 2008.
APA	Miller, J. (2008, September 2). The tyranny of the test: One year as a Kaplan coach in the public schools. *Harper's Magazine,* 35–46.

End-of-Text Citations	
Newspaper	
MLA	Timson, Judith. "Stop All That Multitasking, Study Suggests." *The Toronto Star,* 7 Aug. 2001, p. E2.
CMS	**In footnotes only.**
APA	Timson, J. (2001, August 7). Stop all that multitasking, study suggests. *The Toronto Star,* p. E2.
Journal	
MLA	Collins, Terence, and Melissa Blum. "Meanness and Failure: Sanctioning Basic Writers." *Journal of Basic Writing,* vol. 19, no. 1, 2000, pp. 13–21.
CMS	Collins, Terence and Melissa Blum. "Meanness and Failure: Sanctioning Basic Writers." *Journal of Basic Writing* 19, no. 1 (2000): 13–21.
APA	Collins, T. & Blum, M. (2000). Meanness and failure: Sanctioning basic writers. *Journal of Basic Writing, 19*(1), 13–21.
Electronic Sources	
Entire Web Site	
MLA	National Public Radio. *Morning Edition.* NPR, 14 January 2014, www.npr.org/programs/morning-edition. Accessed 14 Jan. 2014.
CMS	National Public Radio. *Morning Edition.* Accessed January 14, 2014. http://www.npr.org/programs/morning-edition.
APA	National Public Radio. (2014, January). *Morning edition.* Retrieved from NPR web site http://www.npr.org/programs/morning-edition/
Page from a Web Site	
MLA	Abdullah, Mardziah Hayati. "The Impact of Electronic Communication on Writing." *EricDigests.org.* ERIC Clearinghouse on Reading, English, and Communication, 2003, www.ericdigests.org/2004-1/impact.htm. Accessed 13 Oct. 2004.
CMS	Abdullah, Mardziah Hayati. "The Impact of Electronic Communication on Writing." *ERIC Clearinghouse on Reading, English, and Communication.* http://www.ericdigests.org/2004-1/impact.htm.
APA	Abdullah, M. H. (2004, October). The impact of electronic communication on writing. *ERIC Clearinghouse on Reading, English, and Communication.* Retrieved from http://www.ericdigests.org/2004-1/impact.htm

Citation Chart

Citation Chart

End-of-Text Citations	
Online Book	
MLA	Austen, Jane. *Pride and Prejudice.* Project Gutenberg, 2013, www.gutenberg.org/catalog/world/readfile?fk_files=3381939. Accessed 14 Apr. 2014.
CMS	Austen, Jane. *Pride and Prejudice.* London, 1813. http://www.gutenberg.org/catalog/world/readfile?fk_files=3381939.
APA	Austen, J. (1813). *Pride and prejudice.* Project Gutenberg. Retrieved from http://www.gutenberg.org/catalog/world/readfile?fk_files=3381939
Article in an Online Magazine/Newspaper	
MLA	Remnick, David. "Putin and the Exile." *New Yorker.* NewYorker.com, 28 Apr. 2014, www.newyorker.com/talk/comment/2014/04/28/140428taco_talk_remnick. Accessed 28 Apr. 2014.
CMS	Remnick, David. "Putin and the Exile." *New Yorker,* April 28, 2014, accessed April 28, 2014. http://www.newyorker.com/talk/comment/2014/04/28/140428taco_talk_remnick.
APA	Remnick, D. (2014, April 28). Putin and the exile. *New Yorker.* Retrieved from http://www.newyorker.com/talk/comment/2014/04/28/140428taco_talk_remnick
Article in an Online Journal	
MLA	Soliday, Mary. "From the Margins to the Mainstream: Reconceiving Remediation." *College Composition and Communication*, vol. 47, no. 1, 1996, pp. 85–100, www.jstor.org/stable/358275. Accessed 14 Jan. 2014.
CMS	Soliday, Mary. "From the Margins to the Mainstream: Reconceiving Remediation." *College Composition and Communication* 47, no. 1 (1996): 85–100. Accessed January 14, 2014. http://www.jstor.org/stable/358275.
APA	Soliday, M. (1996). From the margins to the mainstream: Reconceiving remediation. *College Composition and Communication, 47*(1). Retrieved from http://www.jstor.org/stable/358275

	End-of-Text Citations
	Film
MLA	*Big Fish.* Directed by Tim Burton, performances by Ewan McGregor, Albert Finney, Jessica Lange, Billy Crudup, and Marion Cotillard, Columbia, 2003.
CMS	McGregor, Ewan, Albert Finney, Jessica Lange, Billy Crudup, and Marion Cotillard. *Big Fish.* DVD. Directed by Tim Burton. Culver City: Sony Home Pictures Entertainment, 2004.
APA	Cohen, B., Zanuck, R. & Jinks, D. (Producer), & Burton, T. (Director). (2003). *Big fish* [Motion picture]. USA: Sony Home Pictures Entertainment.
	Television Program
MLA	"Tabula Rasa." *Criminal Minds: Season 3,* written by Jeff Davis, Dan Sworkin, and Jay Beattie, directed by Steve Boyum, Paramount, 2010.
CMS	Davis, Jeff, Dan Sworkin, and Jay Beattie, "Tabula Rasa." *Criminal Minds,* season 3, episode 19, directed by Steve Boyum, aired May 14, 2008. (Los Angeles: Paramount, 2010), DVD.
APA	Davis, J., Sworkin, D., & Beattie, J. (Writers) & Boyum, S. (Director). (2008). Tabula rasa [Television series episode]. In E.A. Bernero (Producer), *Criminal minds.* Los Angeles, CA: Paramount.
	Sound Recording
MLA	Miranda, Lin-Manuel. *The Hamilton Mixtape,* Atlantic Records, 2016.
CMS	Miranda, Lin-Manuel. *The Hamilton Mixtape.* New York: Atlantic Records, CD. Recorded 2016.
APA	Miranda, L. (2016). *Hamilton Mixtape* [CD]. New York, NY: Atlantic Records.

Conclusion

The guidelines presented in this chapter were put together by style experts in different fields as a means of organizing and codifying secondary research. They differ, as Sarah Scott exhibited in her essay "Writing for the Field of Communication," not only as technical devices but also as rhetorical moves to cue the reader in what has come from outside of the author's own knowledge. Citation styles are important to moving the reading along in an efficient way that also engages the ongoing conversation of the discipline. You will find in your Composition II courses that we privilege disciplinary writing but often we ask you to cite in MLA style. This is simply because, while you will be uncovering the rhetorical conventions and discourses of your discipline, you will be doing so in an English class. As you will see in the next chapter, though, we have designed Composition II assignments to better help you situate yourself in your discipline and move forward as a scholar in that field.

In the following chapter, we walk you through different project overviews used for various assignments by Composition II instructors. Learning to read the genre of the assignment sheet is important to your success as a Composition II student, and your success in this course will determine how prepared you are to enter upper-level classes in your field to engage and produce scholarship. Each of the project overviews presented in the following chapter includes the instructor's notes on the pedagogical imperatives that informed the instructors as they composed the overviews, as well as their own goals for the assignments.

Sample Assignment Overviews

Sample Assignment Overviews

Introduction

The assignment sheet is a genre unto itself. Learning to read this genre so that you can write for the assignment effectively is important for your grade in the class. However, beyond "getting the grade," learning to read situations that involve any evaluation of your performance becomes a necessary skill as you enter the coursework for your major, for graduate school, and later for your career. Instructors here have not only supplied their own materials as examples, but have also noted the pedagogical practices that inform their choices. Knowing what to look for and what drives instructors to create assignments is a skill that will transfer well outside of the composition classroom. As you read the assignment overviews, pay close attention to the elements each assignment sheet outlines as necessary for the completion of the project. The evaluative criteria, or the way in which the instructor assesses your writing, arises from the elements outlined within the assignment sheet. In plainer terms, the assignment sheet acts as a request to which your assignment acts as an answer. Understanding the nature of the request, the way in which the assignment calls for a response, will allow you to craft persuasive projects that appropriately address the particulars of the assignment.

The assignment overviews begin with projects that call upon you to explore disciplinary specific writing (presented in the "Writing in Your Major" and "Case Study" projects) before focusing upon the genres you will use to conduct scholarly research (the Annotated Bibliography and Literature Review). The assignment overviews conclude with projects that prompt you to build upon your research and engage in argumentation (the Position Paper and Researched Argument). Beginning with an exploration of disciplinary specific writing, the first two assignments encourage you to familiarize yourself with disciplinary conventions and discourses. The next two assignments guide you as you develop your own scholarly research, which, in turn, informs your ability to construct the final two assignments, well-researched, valid scholarly arguments.

CRAFTING THE "ANALYSIS OF WRITING IN YOUR MAJOR" PROJECT

Using materials already developed by Dr. Kristi Costello, I developed this assignment to give students an opportunity to review and become familiar with the ways in which the scholarship in their fields operates. Much like a discourse analysis, when writing this particular analysis, students are directed to review scholarship they select and to read for the conventions and vocabularies that they can identify as standard to their fields. Going deeper, students should then articulate why these aspects might exist in that area of study. The idea is that students can then formulate their own understanding of the ways scholarship in their field is constructed and why. This formulation should then better drive them to tease out the underlying structures that inform the knowledge-base and audiences of their disciplines. Because this is an exploratory assignment, I attempt to keep the parameters somewhat loose.

Analysis of Writing in Your Major Assignment Overview

Airek Beauchamp

ENG 1013: Composition II, Arkansas State University

. . . .

Rather than provide the students with directives, I ask students to consider questions that might help them best respond to the assignment sheet. This is an intentional rhetorical act. Asking students questions is not only less directive, allowing them more authorship of their papers, but it also presents the assignment as one of inquiry. At this level of their academic careers, students are not equipped to provide their readers with definitive contours of disciplinary boundaries, but they are able to apprehend and explain the basics of disciplinary discourse. That is exactly what I hope students are able to do after completing this assignment.

An Analysis of Writing in Your Field* is a paper in which you analyze the aspects of appropriate writing in your chosen field of study. This exercise is designed to help you acclimate to the accepted style and format so as to be successful in both upper level/major coursework and ultimately your career. For this assignment, you will examine several credible/exemplary sources published in your field of study and explore and discuss what rhetorical features make them successful. Scholarly articles, reviews, and studies are among the kinds of texts you should explore.

When you write your Analysis assignment, you must explain any concepts you have used to draw meaning and significance from the original texts you examined. Then you should summarize the content of the texts and include contextual background that is essential for the audience to understand before encountering your thesis. Finally, you must compose a thesis that states your opinion concerning why the texts are successful within the context of their particular field. In order to prove the validity of your evaluation, you must take words seriously, know your audience, and read closely so that you can offer strong claims about the text and support those claims with textual evidence.

CONTENT AND PERCEIVED READERSHIP

For this assignment, after considering multiple credible sources, you will choose one source to dissect, analyze, and write about. As you explore your text, consider the following questions:

* What principles of organization govern the text?
* How does the author appeal to the reader's feelings, intellect, and sense of self (i.e., ethos, pathos, logos, and kairos)?

- How does formatting influence the presentation of the writer's ideas?
- What rhetorical strategies does the writer use to affect the way that the message of the text is received?

Once you have responded to the questions above, decide on a unique angle for your analysis.

Your audience is the Arkansas State University first-year community, but remember that you will be writing for a scholarly audience as well. Consider what you know about your peers, faculty, and the authors of this and other sources that you are analyzing as you write. These are intelligent people who may have some knowledge of the information you are covering, but you should not assume that they know everything you do after reading several sources on a particular topic. Accordingly, you will have to explain key concepts and define new terms. You will also have to persuade your readers that you have something valuable to contribute to their intellectual understanding.

STRUCTURE AND STYLE

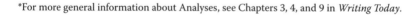

Your Analysis should include a thesis that conveys your evaluation of the text's successfulness within its field or genre, and your analysis of that text should serve as the evidence that supports your evaluation. Refer specifically to the source text in your analysis, using smoothly incorporated summaries, paraphrases, and direct quotations as called for in your paper. Your Analysis of Writing In Your Field should be at least two full pages, but no more than four, and should be written in MLA style. You should create Reference/Bibliography/Works Cited page for your source as appropriate for acceptable writing in your field.

*For more general information about Analyses, see Chapters 3, 4, and 9 in *Writing Today*.

This assignment was adapted for *Writing Today* from an assignment originally published by:

Costello, Kristi. "Rhetorical Assignment Overview—ENG 1003: Composition I, Arkansas State University." *Composition Instructor Network.* Blackboard Learn, Arkansas State University, 2013.

CRAFTING THE "DISCOURSE COMMUNITY CASE STUDY" PROJECT

Terribly clever students will often find that they can respond to many questions concerning language, writing, and persuasion with the indelible, "it depends." What counts as good or effective writing within a discourse community? "It depends." How does one establish credibility with their intended audience? "It depends." Indeed, it does depend, but what often remains unspoken in this response is the what that it depends upon. The what, of course, becomes the actual writing situation, the rhetorical situation within which persuasion occurs. If speaking generally of how writing leads to the aforementioned caveat, then perhaps we can best understand writing by studying how it occurs within **actual** *situations.*

Thus the guiding principle of the Discourse Community Case Study, to study writing as it actually happens, promotes us to explore how writers navigate the rhetorical situations that make up a specific discursive community. If we as writers will have to enter into, and adapt to, the norms of a particular community then we benefit from studying and coming to understand how that community operates. The Case Study makes explicit that which often remains implicit, the norms and conventions of performance that functioning members of a community take for granted. By bringing to the foreground the background practices of a community we gain a more thorough knowledge of how writers within that community write, as well as the influences that constrain their writing, and in turn how we can navigate our own course through the community.

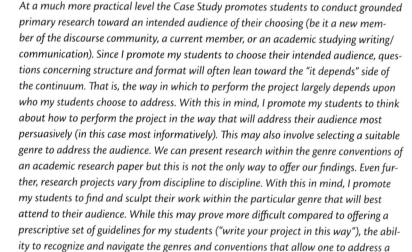

At a much more practical level the Case Study promotes students to conduct grounded primary research toward an intended audience of their choosing (be it a new member of the discourse community, a current member, or an academic studying writing/communication). Since I promote my students to choose their intended audience, questions concerning structure and format will often lean toward the "it depends" side of the continuum. That is, the way in which to perform the project largely depends upon who my students choose to address. With this in mind, I promote my students to think about how to perform the project in the way that will address their audience most persuasively (in this case most informatively). This may also involve selecting a suitable genre to address the audience. We can present research within the genre conventions of an academic research paper but this is not the only way to offer our findings. Even further, research projects vary from discipline to discipline. With this in mind, I promote my students to find and sculpt their work within the particular genre that will best attend to their audience. While this may prove more difficult compared to offering a prescriptive set of guidelines for my students ("write your project in this way"), the ability to recognize and navigate the genres and conventions that allow one to address a particular intended audience becomes an important skill to cultivate as writers within various disciplines.

Discourse Community Case Study Assignment Overview

Zach Warzecka

Composition II, Arkansas State University

This project operates from the premise that we best understand writing and communication when we attend to *the concrete settings within which persuasion occurs*. Rather than attempt to generalize what makes *all* writing "good," or attempt to find overarching genre conventions that might apply to *every* genre, the case study will call upon you to explore how writing and communication play out within the specific environs of a discursive community.

In plainer terms, the Discourse Community Case Study becomes an opportunity for you to study and understand how writing and communication occur within a specific community of writers.

To this end you will conduct primary research that focuses upon how writing and communication unfold within a discourse community of your choosing. You might choose a community that you plan to enter, affording you a more nuanced understanding of how writing works within that community which would inform your entrance into that community, or you could study a community that you find interesting and would like to further explore.

The project requires you to collect data using three methods: observation, interview, and genre analysis. Your project will utilize these methods to attend to the overarching research question: "How does writing and communication occur within this community?"

To attend to this research question, which will lead to more specific research questions once you start your case study, here are a set of guiding lenses (drawn from Rhetorical Genre Studies) that you will use to frame and study your community:

* **Goals and Purposes:** What are the communal goals that your community attempts to fulfill or achieve? Are these goals overtly articulated or does the community address them implicitly? How does writing and communication help to accomplish the discourse community's goals/purposes?

* **Values and Perspectives:** What values or perspectives does the discourse community embody? What *matters* to the discourse community? (I.e., what does the discourse community place value upon and why?)

- **Sub-Communities:** Does the larger discourse community contain smaller sub-communities that have their own more specific/particular goals and purposes? If so, what is the relationship between the larger community and sub-communities? How do the more specific goals and purposes of the sub-community contribute to the discourse community's larger purpose?

- **Social Roles:** What social roles do people within the discourse community play? How are these social roles defined? What are the conventions for the discourse community's social roles? In other words, what are the "rules" that influence how people perform these roles? How do social roles act in relation to one another? Which social roles carry more power/authority and how does this influence their contact with other roles?

- **Genre:** What forms of writing/communication do members of the community employ on a routine basis? What purpose do these genres fulfill? What audiences does each genre address and how do the expectations of that audience influence the composition of the genre? In other words, what are the genre's conventions (the typical or normalized way in which writers compose the genre)? How do different genres operate together (build upon one another) within the community?

- **Writing Technologies:** What technologies does the community utilize in their communicative practices? How do the various technologies that populate the discourse community influence the way in which members write/communicate? Consider any form of technology that might influence communication/writing, including but not limited to: phones, fax machines, computers, computer software, websites, pencils, paper, and so on.

DATA COLLECTION

To understand writing and communication within your discourse community you will necessarily *collect data*. That is, you will conduct primary research that gathers and codes information that you can then analyze. To explore how writing occurs within your discourse community you will employ the following three research methods:

1. Observations

You will observe how the discourse community functions by placing yourself within the setting and taking *notes* (writing down everything that you observe while limiting pre-established ideas or presumptions). For the purposes of the project you will conduct at least one observation of your discourse community.

2. Interviews

Your second research method will call upon you to interview members of the discourse community to gain an insider's perspective on how writing and communication occur within the community. This will entail creating interview questions drawn from the Rhetorical Genre Studies lenses provided above. Remain mindful that each of your interview questions should attend to a particular portion of the overarching research question: "How does writing and communication occur within this community?" Ideally you will conduct multiple interviews but at least one interview should inform the project.

3. Genre Analysis

Gather genres that members of the community routinely use. Genres could show up as physical or digital forms of communication (i.e., an assignment sheet handed out to students within a class or an inter-office message sent electronically). Once you have gathered genres you will analyze them to reveal their conventions (the typical ways in which members of the community write/perform the genre).

For the purposes of explanation I've separated these methods. In practice the findings that you generate from each method will necessarily influence the other two methods. Things you see during your observation will inspire questions that you will ask your interview participants, while interview responses will then influence what you focus upon during your observations. The three methods build upon and work with one another.

STRUCTURE/FORMAT

As with previous projects, I will promote you to consider *who* you would like to address with this research (which may or may not be an academic audience). Indeed, you might consider performing this project as a "how-to" guide for new members of your community. Though we will operate within the larger genre conventions of an "academic primary research project" you will also have the opportunity to address alternative audiences should you see fit—which may change the way you unfold and structure the presentation of your findings.

All of this is to say, you will write your case study in the style and manner that you believe will be most persuasive for your specific intended audience (be that audience academic, non-academic, a new member of the discourse community, or a current member of the community).

Remain mindful that this project's purpose aims to *inform* an audience as to how writing and communication function in the discourse community. You will need to structure and present your research in such a way that your audience comes to understand your discourse community and benefits from this knowledge.

Sample Assignment Overviews

CRAFTING THE "ANNOTATED BIBLIOGRAPHY" PROJECT

Simply reading the name of this assignment can be daunting for someone who has never attempted it before. Depending upon educational backgrounds, some students may have no idea what the words "annotated" or "bibliography" mean separately, let alone how they work as a single concept. At its core, though, an annotated bibliography is nothing more than an amplified list of sources. It is the result of research in a particular topic and is usually only one piece of a larger project which culminates in a research paper or end of term essay, and as such, the goal of creating an Annotated Bibliography is not to state and prove a thesis (as an essay does). Rather, it is to gather sources and evaluate them in terms of usefulness in an argument as well as signs of bias. Students are often surprised to find that Annotated Bibliographies lack staples of composition such as introductions, conclusions, thesis statements, and even transitions between paragraphs. With this in mind, I hope to have written an assignment that turns something terrifyingly alien into an absolutely achievable task.

The assignment sheet is divided into sections, and most of those sections are then further divided into either bullet point or numbered lists. I chose this format because it is similar to that of the assignments my students have been given previously and because Annotated Bibliographies are a great deal of work. If the steps are listed in order, even those who have had no experience with this genre will be able to complete the assignment one step at a time. A third reason for breaking the Annotated Bibliography down as I have is that students often underestimate the amount of time required to complete it. If students realize that this assignment cannot be completed in a single afternoon or even during the day before it is due, since it demands that they actually read and evaluate sources after locating them, then the students are likely to budget their time carefully and produce quality annotations which can actually be of use when they begin to write their researched arguments.

Annotated Bibliography Assignment Overview

Kerri L. Bennett

Composition II, Arkansas State University

. . . .

An Annotated Bibliography is a list of sources on a particular topic that have each been summarized. This is an academic project that is commonly assigned prior to the completion of a larger research project. As such, the sources that are listed in your Annotated Bibliography should be the same sources that are used and cited in your final essay. To be successful in this assignment, students must be able to read and summarize the sources they collect. We will also utilize the following skills:

* researching the library, scholarly databases, and Internet for sources

* gathering sources that pertain to your topic into one list

* indicating how each source will be used or related to your argument (thesis)

* documenting sources using MLA works cited entries

* evaluating sources for credibility and bias

Purpose of the paper: To collect and organize sources that relate to a common theme, to connect those sources to each other and your argument as a whole, and to evaluate the strength of the sources to determine their usefulness.

Audience: An academic audience that includes the authors of the sources and others interested in the issue upon which you are focusing.

STRATEGIES

* *Focus* on a narrowly defined and *arguable* topic.

* *Collect* trustworthy sources such as journal articles, news articles, and magazine articles that are relevant to the topic you have chosen.

* *Organize* your sources alphabetically by the author's last name.

* *Read and Annotate* each source carefully, making sure to note all information that is essential to retaining the overall meaning of the original text.

* *Document* all sources using MLA works cited entries.

* *Summarize* each source accurately, making sure to mention only the most important information in the text. DO NOT include small details that will not affect the overall message of the text.

* *Write* the annotation paragraphs in a *style* that is clear, readable, appropriate to audience, and free from distracting errors in spelling, grammar, and usage.

CONTENT

Your Annotation Paragraphs should include:
1. A summary of the text made up of:
    a. an opening sentence naming the author and alluding to who that person is or what type of source this is,
    b. the thesis/argument/purpose of the source (may also be in the first sentence),
    c. a summary of the logical progression of the source (how does its author get from a to b?),
    d. the best examples or evidence provided in the argument that serve as support for its thesis,
    e. the author's conclusion, which will probably include a suggestion of some sort.
2. An evaluation (your critique of the article) which answers questions such as:
    a. Is the author a credible/authoritative source of information and why?
    b. How did the author build ethos?
    c. Was the logos for the argument convincing?
    d. What types of pathos did the author invoke?
    e. How effective was the author's argument?
    f. Did any fallacies compromise the effectiveness of the author's argument?
    g. Did the author successfully address counterarguments?
    h. Be sure to point out holes in all of the above categories as you see them.
Length should be 3–7 sentences.

FORMAT

Annotated Bibliographies are alphabetized lists made up of multiple entries, each one separate from the others. For each source that you list in your paper, you must include its reference information as well as a paragraph of annotation. Reference information is listed exactly as it would be on a Works Cited page for an MLA paper. The annotation paragraphs that follow the reference information should be indented half an inch to the left of the margin of the second line of the Works Cited entry. All subsequent lines of the paragraph should be aligned with the margin of the second line of the Works Cited entry.

You should read, list (MLA Works Cited entry style), and annotate no fewer than six recent sources and no more than eight. As with other essays written in this class, please follow MLA guidelines for citation and format. Your Annotated Bibliography must be no fewer than two full pages, but no more than six.

CRAFTING THE "LITERATURE REVIEW" PROJECT

I developed this assignment over several years and with the input of many colleagues. The literature review is a genre common to almost every discipline—in some cases, a well-drafted literature review can be published by itself as a guide to the literature in a specific discipline. This assignment in particular gives students a general sense of what a literature review does without necessarily requiring them to engage in the style of any particular discipline. Different disciplines will, to some degree, approach the literature review in different ways.

As I state in the assignment sheet, the literature review the students write in response to this assignment sheet should not advance an argument, nor should the essays contain the authors' points of views. Instead, for this assignment, the author should simply provide the reader with the disciplinary context and history necessary to support the argument the author advances later. Some disciplines, however, use the literature review to begin arguing for a particular approach, point of view, or solution to a perceived problem in the discipline. It is important for students in higher-level classes to find models of literature reviews in their disciplines to better understand the conventions to which they will need to adhere.

Literature Review Assignment Overview

Airek Beauchamp

Composition II Arkansas State University
· ·

Sample Assignment Overviews

A literature review is an informed analysis of a piece of literature through the lens of a certain topic. This is a skill students will be asked to demonstrate in any number of courses and across many disciplines.

In a well-written review, you should move beyond evaluating surface aspects of the text that you "like" or "don't like." Instead, you should analyze a particular piece of literature, and then form an educated opinion concerning the quality of that piece based on the conventions of its genre. After expressing your opinion in a thesis, you should support the thesis with evidence, such as analyses of specific passages from or aspects of the piece. These analyses should "dig deep" and illustrate that you have read the text with a critical eye and thoroughly explored how and why you have come to write the particular thesis you are supporting in this paper. Additionally, you should synthesize your analyses in a cohesive way. In other words, you should explain the deeper meanings and connections you have made within the text in a way that is clear and easy for your readers to understand, so that, ultimately, they will recognize the value of your literature review. This assignment should demonstrate to your audience how it contributes to the disciplinary body of knowledge with which it is engaging.

CONTENT AND AUDIENCE

A literature review is an essay in which you express your informed opinion about a particular source and explain how you came to hold that opinion. In our Composition II course, the assignment requires that you choose five or six credible sources on a related topic, read them critically, and then analyze those texts for meaning as well as explore the way that these texts relate or connect to one another. In other words, how do they fit within the larger rhetorical conversation? You should consider this essay a small piece of the larger project that is your Researched Argument because it is from this literature review that you will begin to form the basis of that essay.

As you write, remember that your audience may not have as much knowledge or understanding of your topic, so it is your responsibility as the author of this literature review to provide enough background information, summary, and explanation for your audience to read your essay with ease and come away with a clear notion of your evaluation of the sources as well as your reasons behind the evaluation.

Sample Assignment Overviews

To help you compose a successful literature review, consider the following questions:

- Why might it be important for your audience to examine these texts? What did you learn from or "take away from" them? Would they be essential reading for anyone interested in this topic, and why or why isn't this the case?

- When examined as a whole, what do they teach us about the genre of which they are a part? How do they fit together in the larger rhetorical conversation they make up? What side of the conversation do they address? What part of the conversation are they ignoring or overlooking? What part is being emphasized too much? What part is being dismissed, perhaps unfairly? What gaps in the literature are evident?

- What role will these sources play in your Researched Argument project? How will they contribute to your beliefs, opinions, and perspectives on the topic you have chosen?

As with other assignments in Composition II, you will write specifically for the Arkansas State University first-year community, but you have an even more specific target within your larger audience, and that is scholars—those who have chosen a particular field to study and research as part of their profession. Therefore, you should be careful to explore the rhetorical conversation in which these texts exist, identify each text's position in that conversation, and trace any connections and/or gaps between them. This will strengthen your ethos as an author. It will also demonstrate your research skills and prove that your evaluation has empirical value and can be trusted.

ORGANIZATION AND FORMAT

There are many ways to organize a literature review depending on your writing style and preferences. Some authors may choose to organize their literature reviews chronologically, while others may prefer thematic or narrative organization styles. Pages 98–101 in *Writing Today* might be helpful when trying to choose a particular style.

Your essay must be no fewer than two full pages and no more than six, and must conform to the current MLA formatting guidelines. You must integrate a variety of sources in your paper, at least five credible sources in all, **three** or more of which must be scholarly sources (published in a scholarly peer-reviewed journal or by a university press, or collected in an anthology of scholarly articles published by a university press).

This assignment has been adapted from one originally published by: Beauchamp, Airek. "Composition II, Arkansas State University: Literature Review." *Composition Instructor Network.* Blackboard Learn, Arkansas State University, 2014.

CRAFTING A "POSITION PAPER" PROJECT

The first inklings of what might become a Position Paper could be born of a casual conversation between friends about a meme that has just gone viral on the internet, an event on a local or national scale that is currently being covered minute-by-minute in the news or on television, or perhaps a political controversy that seems to be at the forefront of everyone's minds. In other words, a Position Paper can focus on any aspect, issue, or event that a writer or an audience might find interesting. If people are talking about something, then writers can take a position on it. Because an Op-Ed is simply an expression of personal opinion printed in a newspaper, a position paper could be seen as a more developed Op-Ed.

I wanted the Op-Ed to serve as the base upon which I constructed my Position Paper Assignment because it is commonly written in Composition I courses at A-State, and if there were similarities between the two assignments, my students could use them as a bridge between an assignment with which they were familiar and one which they had likely never before encountered. For this reason, the assignment sheet that follows has been adapted from an Op-Ed assignment created by Dr. Kristi Costello.

This assignment has been divided into sections so that students who are looking for particular pieces of information about the paper requirements can find answers easily. The first two sections address the Rhetorical Triangle, a necessary step before beginning to write. With a specific purpose, type of content, and audience in mind, writers can more effectively compose working drafts expressing their opinions. Once their ideas are recorded, they can focus on organizing their thoughts in compelling ways and using a particular style when formatting their documents. A list of strategies for success is included at the end of the assignment as a quick way for writers to review the requirements.

Position Paper Assignment Overview

Kerri L. Bennett

Composition II, Arkansas State University

· ·

PURPOSE

A Position Paper is a common type of academic argument that is written after reading about and discussing a particular issue in which you should state and defend your position on the issue as well as illustrate how your opinion relates to similar or opposing opinions about the same issue. When writing your essay, remember that your thesis still needs to be both arguable and supported with details and evidence. Also continue to use transitions, which provide cues for the reader and improve coherence. When writing this paper, concentrate on the following skills:

- collecting information from readings on a particular issue
- choosing an effective organizational strategy
- researching the library and Internet for sources
- documenting sources using MLA in-text citations and a Works Cited page

CONTENT AND AUDIENCE

To focus your Position Paper, you should consider how your own insights add something new to a conversation about fairy tales. Then, reflect on this issue, taking notes on perspectives that you feel are missing or on viewpoints that you feel are incompletely or inaccurately expressed. Even if you are writing about an issue with which you are already familiar, you will want to read several sources pertaining to the issue before you begin writing. Some questions for you to consider as you read your sources are as follows:

- What voices are missing from the conversation?
- Do the writers currently covering this issue seem to be misinterpreting or unfairly representing certain points of view?
- Do the writers currently covering this issue seem to be "getting it right," but still leaving important perspectives out of the conversation?

As you write and revise your position paper, you will integrate relevant research that will allow you to both support your views and distinguish them from the views of others who have written on the issue. Be aware that, typically, strong position papers do not simply take an "either/or" argument, but rather concentrate on nuances about the issue that may have been missed or underdeveloped. In other words, you should say something new rather than rehashing the same tired arguments. Finally, remember that you should develop a strong, well-supported thesis, and that it should address the Arkansas State University first-year community—that is, fellow students and faculty, who are bright, but may have little knowledge of the particular conversation you are entering.

ORGANIZATION AND FORMAT

There are many ways to organize your position paper and, as a class, we will analyze and discuss several readings as well as critical articles concerning them so that you will learn about and be able to articulate a general understanding of the conventions of the genre. Considering these conventions, you will have to decide the best way to arrange your position paper to make your argument clear and persuasive.

Further, to practice the skills necessary for success in Composition II and beyond, you are expected to engage with outside sources in your piece, using summary, paraphrase, and direct quotation as effective and appropriate. You are also required to incorporate in-text parenthetical citations and develop an end-of-text Works Cited page, which includes *all* sources used and cited within your position paper. You should read and cite (on the Works Cited) no fewer than *three recent sources*. As with other essays written in this class, please follow MLA guidelines for citation and format. *Your position paper must be no fewer than three full pages, but no more than four.*

STRATEGIES FOR COMPOSING A SUCCESSFUL POSITION PAPER

- Develop your argument by defending your thesis. Illustrate how it relates to the positions of your sources. Use clearly stated reasons and strong, relevant evidence. These reasons should represent sound logic and help strengthen your ethos as a scholarly author. The evidence supporting these reasons may be drawn from the class readings as well as outside written and digital sources that have been approved.

- Organize your paper in a way that effectively communicates your message to your readers so that it is easy to follow, and presents your thesis (position) in relation to those of the source authors.

- Write in a style that is clear, readable, and mostly free from distracting errors in spelling, grammar, and usage.

- Cite all outside sources (both written and digital sources) using MLA in-text citations and a Works Cited page.

This assignment adapted from:

Costello, Kristi. "Opposite Editorial Assignment Overview—ENG 1003: Composition I, Arkansas State University." *Composition Instructor Network*. Blackboard Learn, Arkansas State University, 2013.

Sample Assignment Overviews

CRAFTING A "RESEARCHED ARGUMENT" PROJECT

Though I had been teaching Composition before meeting Dr. Kristi Costello, and had therefore produced my own assignment sheets previously, I always received a myriad of questions, the answers to which I thought had been clearly addressed in my assignment instructions. When she became Director of Composition at A-State, she suggested that the instructors share their assignments with one another online. To that end, she uploaded an assignment very like the one you see printed below. I liked the way information was organized and the clearly expressed expectations. The assignment was also much less visually intimidating than my nearly full page of solid text, so I began using my own version of it in my classes. As indicated in the source information, I have made specific adaptations to her original assignment and tailored it to my personal teaching style and the construction of my particular Composition II courses.

This assignment sheet is divided into three sections, the first two of which form the Rhetorical Triangle. Purpose, content, and audience are three aspects that a writer must consider before ever beginning the first word of an essay, and since these are important initial considerations, they are addressed before anything else. Included in the second section is a list of questions that are aimed at helping writers understand the rhetorical conversations they are entering and their own opinions and perspectives within that conversation. The third section is dedicated to organization and format, and it also contains a list of questions. These are meant to show writers the most efficient and understandable way to present the contents of their messages to their readers. Because a researched argument written for Composition II is necessarily more complex and demanding than a similar assignment written for Composition I, I hope that the detailed explanation of my expectations for this assignment will provide clear answers to the student writers and leave them with the information they need to begin this assignment without confusion or apprehension.

Researched Argument Assignment Overview

Kerri L. Bennett

Composition II, Arkansas State University

WHY A RESEARCHED ARGUMENT?

Making an argument—expressing a point of view on a subject and supporting it with reasons and evidence—is often the aim of academic writing, even if the word "argument" is never used. Your college instructors may assume that you know this and thus may not explain the importance of arguments to you in class. Someone, somewhere, has debated most material you learn in college at some time. Even when the material you read or hear is presented as simple "fact," it may actually be one person's interpretation of a set of information. In your writing, instructors may call on you to question that interpretation and defend it, refute it, or offer some new view of your own. In short, in writing assignments, you will almost always need to do more than just present information that you have gathered or regurgitate facts that were discussed in class. You will need to select a point of view and provide evidence to develop your *own* considered argument.

STRUCTURE AND PROPOSED READERSHIP

In a Researched Argument, you should examine a variety of sources, including scholarly articles, which discuss a range of perspectives on contemporary issues being debated in various cultures, including academic disciplines. You should put these credible and scholarly articles into conversation with each other, analyzing how writers offer diverse perspectives in different ways. As a new member of the academic community, you should find where your voice, perspective, and argument fit into the existing conversation. So, unlike a research report (a popular high school genre that summarizes or explains ideas), a Researched Argument asks writers to interpret a wide spectrum of perspectives, *and* offer creative insights.

This assignment asks you to build on your source citation and argumentation skills, engage in critical examination of texts, perform careful observation and develop your voice, and work within the broad and diverse conventions of scholarly research. You may choose to use in-class readings as a touchstone for your writing, and/or expand on an issue you've already written about in this course or others. Whatever you decide, you should investigate an issue that you are genuinely interested in learning more about.

When you find an issue you would like to focus on, ask yourself the following questions:

- What are the core controversies at the heart of the issue?
- What do I need to define or explain to readers so they can make sense of the issue? What sources will I use and what gaps are there in these sources?
- What information am I seeking from additional sources to fill these gaps?
- Do sources agree on an issue? Disagree? Are they somewhere in between?
- How do I respond to these sources? Given my own life experiences with or analysis of the issue, what do I think?

As with other assignments in this course, you will write for a specific audience: the Arkansas State University first-year community, but particularly scholars within this community. As such, you should explain important concepts to your readers (who are intellectually curious, but who have different knowledge bases and areas of expertise); you should also seek to persuade readers that your perspectives are worth considering.

GENRE CONVENTIONS

As you begin your research and brainstorming, look to the readings that we have examined in class and other academic arguments to help imagine an appropriate structure. Consider the following questions:

- What kinds of research questions are writers trying to answer?
- How do they begin and end their pieces?
- How do they use evidence, including summary, paraphrase, quotation, and analysis?
- How do they signal that they are moving on to another portion of their argument?
- How do they show their willingness to listen to and engage with alternative viewpoints?

Once you have a general understanding of the conventions of researched argumentation, you will work to arrange your ideas in ways your readers will recognize: develop a clear thesis; demonstrate a range of perspectives on the issue; analyze and complicate those perspectives; and offer new insights to the academic conversation. If you are just documenting and summarizing sources, you may be merely writing a report. If you are summarizing or drawing on sources revolving around a common focus and then engaging with each of them related to an argument you support in your thesis statement, you are probably writing a Researched Argument.

Your essay must be no fewer than six full pages and no more than eight, and must use MLA style formatting conventions. You must incorporate (embed or "sandwich") a variety of sources into your paper. This means that they must have diverse origins, some coming from print media and others from digital media. All cannot come from websites, and none can come from Wikipedia. You must **use** and **cite** at least *six* credible sources total, at least **three** of which must be scholarly sources (published in a peer-reviewed journal or by a university press, or collected in an anthology of scholarly articles published by a university press).

This assignment adapted from:

Costello, Kristi. "Researched Argument Assignment Overview—ENG 1003: Composition I, Arkansas State University." *Composition Instructor Network.* Blackboard Learn, Arkansas State University, 2013.

Source: https://www.pexels.com/photo/hand-drowning-paper-cafe-28216/

Introduction

Having provided you with examples of assignment sheets, and a peek into the pedagogical drives that informed our composition of the assignments, it is time for you to see student writing in action. Each of the essays in this chapter was provided by actual students in Composition II classes on the Arkansas State campus. Along with each assignment, we have asked the author to provide a brief bio and writing advice for future students (you!). We have structured this chapter to reflect the same order in which we presented the sample assignment sheets in the previous chapter: beginning with assignments that familiarize students with the discourses and conventions of their chosen field, followed by assignments that guide students in developing scholarly research, and concluding with the assignments that ask students to develop sound academic arguments in their chosen disciplines.

Reviewing the work of fellow Comp II students may provide you with a more concrete sense of how to navigate writing in Composition II. Analyze these examples with an eye for the writer's strengths within the project—ways in which the project functions effectively within the genre conventions of the assignment—as well as the aspects you would address or incorporate differently because they are less persuasive and in need of further development or revision. While you won't replicate the work of these students, you can learn from their texts, building upon, "stealing," and transforming the elements of the projects to inform your own work within the course. In plainer terms, read these examples for what works well and what you might change within your own projects.

The following student writers offer examples of how to respond to Composition II writing assignments:

Joseph Thomas—"Emotionless: Writing in the Lines" Analysis of Writing in Your Major

- Joseph's Analysis of Writing in Your Major examines the ways in which scholars in Computer Science pursue disciplinary conversations.

Karis Evans—"The Importance of Global Journalism" Literature Review

- Karis' Literature Review provides the reader with an overview of how the scholarly literature in Journalism contributes specifically to the topic of global journalism.

AUSTIN MAY—"THE GREAT DEBATE" LITERATURE REVIEW

- In his Literature Review Austin discusses the literature surrounding the certification requirements of people in the engineering field and why these certifications are (or are not) necessary.

SETH PRICE—"WHAT DO STANDARDIZED TESTS ACCOMPLISH?" OP-ED

- In his Op-Ed Seth argues that academic standardized testing is ineffective.

GARRET HARLOW—"AGRICULTURE: SAVING CIVILIZATION" RESEARCHED ARGUMENT

- Garret, in his Researched Argument, studies the state of modern agriculture in America and argues that we have the ability to end world hunger.

NATHAN WALTERS—"WILL YOU SETTLE FOR THE NORM?" ARGUMENTATIVE ESSAY

- In his Argumentative Essay, Nathan argues that the negative side effects of fast food consumption should keep consumers away from fast food products.

PATRICK TRIBBETT—"MONSTERS IN THE MEDIA" POSITION PAPER

- Patrick's Position Paper compares and contrasts the ways in which Western society has constructed the concept of the monster, and how this same concept was used against people with HIV/AIDS.

GABRIELLE RANNALS—"WHAT AMERICANS LACK IN SCIENTIFIC KNOWLEDGE" INFOGRAPHIC ARGUMENT

- Gabrielle uses the genre of the Infographic to make a visual argument that discusses the dangers of a citizenship with limited scientific literacy.

JOSEPH THOMAS

Joseph was born in Jonesboro, AR, and is a sophomore here at A-State pursuing a degree in Computer Science. In high school, writing was not his forte; however, he excelled in math and science. Composition I and II changed his writing skills for the better and the ways in which the ASU Writing Center, professors, and his fellow class peers helped him develop and improve his writing cannot be overlooked.

Joseph recommends that all students utilize the Writing Center to their greatest ability, whether to brainstorm ideas or revise a paper for any class. While there's no such thing as a perfect piece of writing, it's important to constantly improve your work.

THE ASSIGNMENT: ANALYSIS OF WRITING IN YOUR MAJOR ESSAY

The Analysis of Writing in Your Major is designed to familiarize students with the genre of the research article. This assignment is in some ways a more focused and thorough version of both the rhetorical analysis and discourse analysis in that it asks students to recognize and identify patterns in their discipline's scholarly research and, further, to note the conventions and discourses of the genre of the disciplinary research paper. The goal is, when the student has identified how a research paper works she might then be better to relate it to why it works that way. Identifying genre, conventions, and discourses are crucial to academic success, but even more crucial is understanding how these factors influence how knowledge is created and disseminated in the disciplines. Students are instructed to research and write to the field of study they have chosen to give them a solid introduction to this scholarship and research before they enter upper-level classes in their major. As Joseph plans to go into the field of Computer Science, he has centered his essay around this literature.

Emotionless: Writing in the Lines

Joseph Thomas

Overview of Writing in Your Major Essay:
Written in Airek Beauchamp's Composition II Class

In reviewing the writing style used by scholars in the discipline of Computer Science, I found a better understanding of how one writes in my field of study to make a successful scholarly article. When reviewing articles and journals in the discipline of Computer Sciences, I soon discovered the styles authors used in the piece by: defining and targeting their audience, their use of rhetorical appeals (logos, ethos and pathos), and how they balanced them out, organization of the paper, and diction used in order to make their paper successful. The overall style, organization, and use of words contributed into making their article scholarly. Likewise, their use of rhetorical appeals, diction, and structure also helped to drive their papers further toward being scholarly. The papers were excellent in providing a literature review/summary at the beginning of the article to inform the reader what the article is about and consists of; without this, the article would not convey what the piece is about and firmly ground the readers' understanding of what they are going to read.

The articles by Abhinav Gupta and Mahesh Khandke provide excellent examples that can be used as templates to dissect and analyze writing in the discipline of Computer Science as the authors used rhetorical appeals, organization, descriptive and detailed diction to form their papers into professional articles on topics within the field of Computer Science. Their papers provide logical and formal styles of writing and detailed reports of their topics. Gupta and co-writer Thilagam go into detail of attacks on the web and describe those attacks more in-depth and what can be done. However, Khandke and co-writers Kadam and Mangore talk about algorithms and concerns of reservations and Optical Grid (31).

As I read the articles, I distinguished the rhetorical appeals used in the papers, which consisted of logos, ethos, pathos, and kairos. The articles consist of logos and some ethos, in that ethos was indirectly convincing readers of their credibility to the paper. However, the ethos used is reliant upon the use of logos, the logical standpoint of the paper, by establishing their claims through logic. The authors' papers that I analyzed excluded the use of pathos. Kairos revolves around timeliness of when an author places text or information at the precise time of when that information would best suit the paper. Kairos falls under the organization of a paper in this instance, as the authors format their papers and introduce their topics in order of what is best. For example, Bolanos, Gonzalez, Arismendi, and Gonza's *A Methodologies and Processes Language for the Software Industry*, includes the context of the topic toward the beginning. This is essential to provide the readers with an understanding of the topic.

The organization of these academic journals are similar to many English papers, as these pieces give a summary of what the article or journal will discuss. These are broken down into headings and subheadings in an organized fashion that allows them to dissect and dive into more detail of what that section is about instead of cramming the information into a multitude of paragraphs that may have readers confused about what is actually together. They are quite methodical in providing what they are talking about here and what the reader will expect to find in that part of the reading. The article by Gupta and Thilagam entitled "Attacks on Web Services Need to Secure XML on Web" introduces terms as headings and also uses details to explain the terms more in-depth. One example in "Attacks on Web Services Need to Secure XML on Web" is when they list the bolded subheading, "3.1.1 SQL Injection:" then describes/defines it as, "SQL injection is an attack that generally occurs with databases. In this input, query provided to the database is modified in such a way to alter the output of the query as per the attacker requirement [11]" (qtd. in Wichers and Manico 2). While the authors use logos, ethos and kairos, they omit pathos as the article is more factual.

As the author leaves out pathos in programming itself, we leave out the emotional appeal of writing because the paper was not one to be driven with emotion. Any emotional use of diction in the paper will shift the piece away from a professional report over their topic. To offer a comparison, no one has ever witnessed a computer cry (though they may fry), whereas in writing in the field of Computer Science, the emotion is left out and not used as a tool to convey what the writer is discussing. The lack of pathos is demonstrated because it has no "use value," as it would be called in writing code, since there are little to no instances in which "flowery language" is used when writing academically in the field. Writing for Computer Science in programming reveals the cold hard facts and commands to a computer and the computer soon regurgitates the results the programmer is looking for. This makes logos more involved and the main rhetorical appeal used, as Computer Science is composed of logical and intellectual styles of writing, while the use of pathos may discredit the author's article as well as their use of logos and ethos.

The overall diction is excellent in the journals considering it is very detailed and descriptive. Even with the use of jargon in the world of Computer Science, authors often describe and define any words that would not be as clear to other people who are unfamiliar with the jargon used in

Computer Science. Many words portray different meanings when used in other subjects. One example of jargon used in Clary Thomas' "Horizons in Computer Science Research," is located in the introduction, revealing "The use of various computational and modeling languages has allowed software engineers to make the abstractions of ideas that can be expressed using natural language (NL)" (153). This jargon would leave people who are illiterate in computing confused of what natural language and abstractions mean in this paper. Since jargon can be abundantly used by some authors, their targeted audience is more narrowed.

The author's target audience was mainly focused on people who read intellectual, factual, and logical articles and who also love to learn and read about what is going on. The papers that I've read and analyzed are report or research articles on studies in the field. These articles are not often read by someone in agriculture, but more so focuses on the technological fields, such as STEM (Science, Technology, Engineering, and Mathematics), but is not limited to any sort of field.

I've come to the understanding that pathos is important in the fact that it needs to be left out, and logos is the main rhetorical appeal to be used when writing in the field of Computer Science. It is based on showing reports and/or discussing one's finding in a logical, intellectual, and formal writing style that is built toward the audience of computing minded people, as it is filled with jargon for Computer Science majors and other technological fields of study (it does not limit one to write for a general audience). Analyzing these papers in the field of Computer Science allows one to provide a template pertaining to how they can write with the knowledge of the styles of organization, rhetorical appeals, diction, and targeting the correct audience in order to write a successful paper in the discipline.

Works Cited

Clary, Thomas S. *Horizons in Computer Science Research*. 9th ed., Nova Science Publishers, 2015, pp. 151–158.

Gupta, Abhinav, and Santhi Thilagam P. "Attacks on Web Services Need to Secure XML on Web." *Computer Science & Engineering: An International Journal*, vol. 3, no. 5, Oct. 2013, pp. 1–11.

Khandke, Mahesh, Ganesh M. Kadam, and Anirudh K. Mangore. "Failure Recovery Using RSWF Algorithm for Advanced Reservation in Optical Grid." *Computer Science & Engineering: An International Journal*, vol. 2, no. 6, Dec. 2012, pp. 31–40.

Karis Evans

Karis is a sophomore majoring in Multimedia Journalism and minoring in Political Science. She worked diligently on her essay, as she found the topic not only interesting but also germane to her future career.

The Assignment: Literature Review

The Literature Review is a genre shared by almost all disciplines, though there may be vast variations across disciplines in form and function of the genre. In many disciplines the literature review is a stand-alone piece of writing meant to maintain currency in the field regarding specific areas of research. In these disciplines the literature review has little to do with argument and instead the material is focused almost solely on building a solid history of the subject at hand and scaffolding it in a way that allows the author to build to the most current material. This form of the literature review is invaluable to researchers who are attempting to enter the disciplinary conversation without having the extensive background required.

I use the genre of the literature review in Composition II as a means of developing an argument. While I ask my students to refrain from using this assignment to explicitly make an argument, often the developing argument they will make becomes somewhat clear to the reader as the assignment draws to a close. Rather than an explicit argument, though, the literature review is to familiarize the reader with the foundational literature on a particular topic— who has said what, when, and to whom. The literature review differs from an annotated bibliography in that it doesn't isolate sources but instead puts them in conversation with each other. By the end of a successful literature review, the reader should have a good idea of the background the author is discussing, from where the conversation began to where it is now. In the examples that follow, Karis offers a thorough review of the literature on the impact globalization has on journalism and Austin provides us with a discussion of the rigorous processes one must pass through to become certified as an engineer and the logic behind these processes.

It is interesting to note the change in my assignment sheet throughout the years. Karis was a later student, while Austin was one of the first Composition II courses I taught at the A-State campus. Earlier on I constructed this assignment in a way that asked students to reflect on the rhetorical choices the authors made and how or why these choices were effective. You can see this requirement reflected in Austin's essay. Due to this requirement the assignment, though in many ways the same, produced very different results in student writing.

The Importance of Global Journalism

Karis Evans

Literature Review Essay:
Written in Airek Beauchamp's Composition II Class

Minor state elections in the United States may never appear to be important on the national radar. However, while examining the crises outside the borders, every issue has the potential to be internationally significant. Due to globalization, countries hold one another accountable economically and politically. Journalists covering stories on the global spectrum have several aspects to consider in what issues are to be included for citizen speculation, such as relevance and close connections to the countries being discussed. Furthermore, they need to focus more on what is happening globally to properly inform the public since the events could be closer to home than the general population may realize.

Global journalism is a very broad subject, and it's imperative to understand what it encompasses. Peter Berglez presented research on international journalism and how the style contrasts to domestic journalism used within countries. However, one definition isn't possible to pin down due to the constantly changing state of globalization. Berglez wrote, "...global journalism ought to be the kind of journalistic practice which 'makes it into an everyday routine to investigate how people and their actions, practices, problems, life conditions etc. in different parts of the world are interrelated'" (Berglez 846). Reporting on the global scale includes seeking out connections between different cultures and people, because the audience would then be able to understand the social background and what may have attributed to the event or disaster. Using the global outlook would allow journalists to seek commonalities so they could provide information on pandemic threats, transnational processes, and unrestricted economic flow (Berglez 847). Journalism is always examining relations between people and practices, and the same practices are used on the global scale.

The media, however, may highlight one focus or country over others in the examination of global news. Brandon Gorman and Charles Seguin dive into the subject of certain foreign leaders in media coverage, and what makes some countries more important than others. They approach the subject from two different viewpoints: realist and liberal. From realist traditions, the world thrives from the logic of self-help and survival, and liberal views would see the world as cooperative and interdependent (Gorman and Seguin 776). The two scholars work to identify the reasons some countries get more air time over others. Applying the realist view,

"The most powerful countries are the most important in the international system, and events that can potentially alter the global balance of power, such as wars are central features" (Gorman and Seguin 777). This perspective would reveal that the only news-worthy stories on the global spectrum would be those that have greater possibility of affecting the home country. However, with the liberal view, "[S]tates that are prominent within international organizations are thus seen as the most influential in the international system, and processes that increase connectivity among states, such as trade, are central features" (Gorman and Seguin 777). As a result of this stance, the media coverage of partners will interconnect the countries from their economic ties. With either perspective, global news coverage has the tendency to neglect countries that don't play major first-hand roles in the betterment of the United States, economically or politically.

From the changing technological world, the way citizens get their news has broadened to the use of the internet. George Lazaroiu wrote about the expansion of journalistic styles due to the new medium. He wrote, "… although online journalism is still dominated by breaking news coverage, new genres are emerging that differentiate it more and more from old journalism" (Lazaroiu 165). Traditional news sources such as BBC, CNN, and the *New York Times* are prime examples of informants that use the internet to post their breaking news stories. However, bias is a recurring issue for media when looking at global news, so the new genres could be used as an advantage to remain equal in reporting news from different countries. Lazaroiu wrote on the issue, stating, "Media skew has serious ramifications for people's understanding of and perceptions of a hazard situation or disastrous event. Internet media may compensate for the basing influence of capital concentration in the print and broadcast journalism" (Lazaroiu 166). The alternative news sources would be able to write on an event and not worry about viewership numbers as print and broadcast media does. In Gorman's writing, the issue of focusing on main contributors to the US was discussed, and part of the reason is that citizens will pay attention to news of countries they recognize. When they don't show interest in certain international stories, print and broadcast media don't give those pieces as much air time as breaking news stories. The Internet gives the opportunity to dive into those global events to provide in depth features through that medium.

Globalization plays a major role in the world today, including media and news coverage. Simon Cottle studied how distant disasters feel close to home due to globalization. As a result of efforts to connect with other countries, every fundamental problem is globally oriented and invigorated (Cottle 78). Every natural disaster, rebellion, or political conflict would always hold the possibility of retaliation from both allies and enemies. For example, natural disasters or conflicts surrounding a region could lead to the advancement of war aims from opponents (Cottle 80). Cottle further examines the effects of globalization on journalism techniques, and the lack of coverage on international disasters. He wrote, "…[networks] have yet to recognize global crises more theoretically as critical drivers in ongoing processes of globalization…" (80). He reveals, through several references to scholars, that journalists must look at global crises from a new perspective to fully be able to cover the global stories efficiently for their audience.

Further research reveals how the audience reacts to the news of distant disasters and human suffering. Maria Kyriakidou studied how media coverage of distant suffering is perceived by the audience. The study was carried out by having focus groups read news articles through different mediums and recording their reactions to the stories. Before revealing the results of the study, she first identifies that mediation is the key concept in understanding the inclusion of international media in the news. She wrote of the practices of producers providing social, economic, and political context to the images used, and that such practices "cannot be taken for granted on the basis of the global dissemination of media cultural products" (Kyriakidou 486). This practice was significant in the focus groups in order for the participants to fully comprehend the disasters discussed. Cosmopolitanism was discussed as respondents made connections with the suffering as "empathy towards the victims, as an awareness of a global community of viewers, and finally, as a responsibility for the alleviation of the suffering" (Kyriakidou 487). As the participants were made aware of how much others were suffering, their first instinct is to help instead of turn a blind eye since they aren't close in proximity to the issue.

The research presented gives several different aspects of globalization and covering global news. One major underlying theme throughout the scholarly articles is that news on the global scale is significant for all people to be aware of. The media offers a number of news sources for people to take advantage of, but it's their choice to acknowledge the world around them. Not only are citizens supposed to know what is happening in their town, county, or state, but they should look beyond their country's borders to examine the interdependence of the global system.

Works Cited

Berglez, Peter. "What Is Global Journalism?" *Journalism Studies*, vol. 9, no. 6, 2008, pp. 845–858. *Communication & Mass Media Complete.* Accessed 11 Mar. 2016.

Cottle, Simon. "Taking Global Crises in the News Seriously: Notes from the Dark Side of Globalization." *Global Media & Communication*, vol. 7, no. 2, 2011, pp. 77–95. *Communication & Mass Media Complete.* Accessed 11 Mar. 2016.

Gorman, Brandon, and Charles Seguin. "Reporting The International System: Attention To Foreign Leaders In The US News Media, 1950–2008." *Social Forces*, vol. 2, 2015, p. 775. *Opposing Viewpoints in Context.* Accessed 11 Mar. 2016.

Kyriakidou, Maria. "Imagining Ourselves Beyond The Nation? Exploring Cosmopolitanism In Relation To Media Coverage Of Distant Suffering." *Studies In Ethnicity & Nationalism*, vol. 9, no. 3, 2009, p. 481. Accessed 11 Mar. 2016.

Lāzāroiu, George. "Global Journalism And The Heterogeneity Of Internet Communication." *Journalism Studies*, vol. 10, 2009, pp. 165–170. *Communication & Mass Media Complete.* Accessed 11 Mar. 2016.

AUSTIN MAY

Austin is a Junior Finance and Accounting major from Little Rock, Arkansas. As might be evident by his essay, in his first year he was an Engineering major, thus his Literature Review reflects on the nature of writing for that specific discipline. He has enjoyed all of his time spent at Arkansas State University and hopes to share more great experiences with his peers during his remaining few semesters. He plans to graduate in May of 2018 and pursue a career in banking, specializing in personal wealth management. As a student, Austin challenges everyone to take pride in their work since the results can and mostly will be a direct reflection of the student.

When writing, Austin takes time to look into his work from many different perspectives and likes to get insight from others who review his work. He feels that the writing center has helped him take different approaches at writing papers and feels he is more efficient at closing the gap between what the writer is trying to say and what the reader is pulling from the text. He feels that knowledge is the greatest tool we have and everyone should view education as a useful and necessary means to growing oneself.

THE ASSIGNMENT: LITERATURE REVIEW

The Literature Review is a genre shared by almost all disciplines, though there may be vast variations across disciplines in form and function of the genre. In many disciplines the literature review is a stand-alone piece of writing meant to maintain currency in the field regarding specific areas of research. In these disciplines the literature review has little to do with argument and instead the material is focused almost solely on building a solid history of the subject at hand and scaffolding it in a way that allows the author to build to the most current material. This form of the literature review is invaluable to researchers who are attempting to enter the disciplinary conversation without having the extensive background required.

It is interesting to note the change in my assignment sheet throughout the years. Karis was a later student, while Austin was one of the first Composition II courses I taught at the A-State campus. Earlier on I constructed this assignment in a way that asked students to reflect on the rhetorical choices the authors made and how or why these choices were effective. You can see this requirement reflected in Austin's essay. Due to this requirement the assignment, though in many ways the same, produced very different results in student writing.

The Great Debate

Austin May

Literature Review:
Written for Airek Beauchamp's Composition II Class

When considering professions and how they affect people, we may initially think about occupations in medicine and business. Fewer, however, give thought to the field of engineering and how directly it impacts people's lives. Every day, billions of commuters travel across bridges but how many recognize the thought, planning, and effort put into each detail of the work of art? Given the important function of this art however, as well as the potential for disaster should it fail, some are concerned about the current qualifications—or lack thereof—required for students to become engineers.

Over the years, the requirements to be an engineer have completely shifted. Up until about the 1950s, anyone with an above average ability to solve problems and ingenuity could easily prove themselves worthy of building structures. Back then "engineers" were simply farmers trying to solve problems on their own land, cheaply but efficiently building bridges, structures, and other devices used for farming. Calling that kind of person an engineer today is laughable; now we have to earn the title through strenuous and time consuming classes just for a bachelor's degree in any field of engineering. And as our understanding of science and physics increases, many people believe the requisite qualifications to become an engineer should increase, as well.

Is four years of college enough to prepare a person for the responsibility of millions of commuters' lives? To become a civil engineer specializing in structures, all that is needed is a bachelor's degree and a professional engineering license. To acquire a PE license one must pass an eight hour test which "comprises engineering-specific skills [including how to] identify, formulate, and solve technical/engineering problems, ... use appropriate/modern tools, ... and apply knowledge of mathematics, science, engineering" (Blom 9).

This strikes an argument amongst those unfamiliar with engineering and licenses. Here Blom did well on hitting the key points of what the test consists of, although he did not go into further detail about what exact subjects and types of questions lie within the test. If revised, Blom would likely need to further support the statements by telling the reader the laundry list of steps just to qualify to take the test, as well as more deeply investigate the test itself. This is where the argument begins. Most think that since

bachelor's degrees are one of the most acquired degrees by college students, engineers with bachelor's degrees fall short of the proper knowledge and training needed to design and construct a structure meant to support heavy vehicles and lives of the drivers operating them.

We must also consider whether qualifications are examined thoroughly by the institutions responsible for finding and hiring engineers to build structures. "In one study of 149 firms hiring scientists and engineers fresh from college, it was found that for 80% of the firms, the personality factor was of primary importance. It was more important than the individual's course of training, work experience, and college grades" (French 270). Here the author, French, uses research from a study done to prove a point being made in his article. French adds a statistic found during a study to help attract the reader's attention and also give his side of the argument more concrete support. French argues from the opposite side of the fence but gives the readers something that sounds more credible. Thinking this way gives the writer the ability to add an even more solid foundation of text to the articles read and gives him/her the advantage to sway people's minds in the direction of the argument.

Of course, we should take into account the course work, time, money and natural problem solving abilities engineers have. These may speak volumes themselves and could easily persuade some readers that even basic engineers are actually over qualified. This article does an excellent job of arguing how well rounded an engineer with "just" a bachelor's degree really is by stating that to receive a BSCE one must complete the program which has the aspiration to train the students to become critical, conscious and committed engineering scientists in a spirit of liberal examination from a non-dogmatic and pluralistic point of view towards society and the chosen engineering specialization field, with emphasis on the sustainability of the solutions, ethics and awareness of the implications to the environment (Van Biesen 221).

Here, Van Biesen uses extremely impressive diction which not only makes himself sound more intelligent, but also shows how educated he is in the field. Biesen talks about two points of view (non-dogmatic and Pluralistic) when approaching the path of not only gaining a bachelor's degree in civil engineering but also further applying the degree in the working world. He then goes on to point out that gaining a bachelor's degree will also teach the engineer the importance of "ethics and awareness" when working with different environments.

Biesen did a fine job breaking down the attributes an engineer will gain and explaining the whole process of engineer qualifications. He used in-depth research and incredible diction, but also told the readers the mental attributes and morals that are gained with just a four year degree. The

writer also shows strong bias towards the appreciation and commitment of basic level engineers which helps support the argument presented in the piece.

Looking at it from the other side means exploring the minds of those who think engineers are under qualified in their fields of expertise. A prime example is the collapse of the Hoan Bridge many years ago due to "the geometric arrangement of the lateral bracing connection into the web of the girders that created a highly constrained condition and prevented yielding of the girder web when overloaded" (Hesse 1). Hesse then follows with "This paper describes the failure and its causes and suggests engineering lessons to be learned. The unique details of the failure offer the opportunity to promote critical thinking and problem solving at levels appropriate to undergraduate students" (Hesse 1). Hesse shows readers that he has a deep level of understanding about the function of bridges by stating specific parts and how they work. He goes on to further his argument by stating that "undergraduates" can promote their skills as engineers, which in a way manipulates readers into thinking that undergraduate students are responsible for the collapse of the bridge solely due to being under qualified. The writer can be seen using accurate descriptions of what actually happened to further his credibility on the subject. Hesse then makes his argument clear by stating who can learn from the mistakes made.

I believe that engineers should stand out as the one of, if not the most, ethical people in the workforce showing that not only do they take pride in their work but also apply themselves when learning as well. It is stated very clearly in the Engineering preamble "Engineers must perform under a standard of professional behavior that requires adherence to the highest principles of ethical conduct" emphasizing that being an ethical worker and thinker is the backbone of the engineering world (Burgess 1). Implicit in this statement are the extremely challenging four years of school work to acquire a bachelor's degree as well as the preparation needed to take and pass the Professional Engineering exam. It is safe to say that engineers are easily well qualified to hold the responsibility of building a structure that will hold and support human lives.

Engineering is, and always will be, a changing process due to the steady inflow of new research and the many ways the world is constantly changing. This is not a bad thing though. Since engineering is always evolving, this means that the modern-day engineer has a very small chance of making mistakes that an engineer even fifteen years ago could make. When it comes to structural engineering, the methods and plans of building bridges have come an astonishingly long way from our ancient, first attempts. The minimum requirement of today's structural engineer isn't even imaginable to an engineer of the 1950s. This is mostly due to the thousands of changes and laws set in place with only one purpose: keeping the public safe.

As an engineering student myself, I can personally attest to the qualifications of a four year degree. Though only in the second semester of my freshman year, I have already taken mathematics and science courses that some will not take until junior or senior year. Success lies within the student's ability to work and learn. If one has good work ethic and is responsible then that person will one day be a very good engineer. If one does not have good work ethic and is not very responsible, the engineering program will more than likely weed that person out. Reason is, engineering classes are all building classes meaning that to go on to higher level courses, one must actually learn and master the prerequisites. This means that unless one is a modern day Einstein, there is no way possible that one can slide through the cracks to obtain a four year degree in any type of engineering.

Passing the Professional Engineering exam is another feat which most cannot conquer. This exam is eight hours long and covers almost every key subject involved in engineering. To be precise, only about twenty percent of all graduated students actually hold a Professional Engineering license; only the most qualified engineers only holding a bachelor's degree are the ones that we rely on to build the structures and bridges that support our everyday transportation and livelihoods. Most do not even realize that a prerequisite to taking the Professional Engineering exam is another eight hours exam called the Fundamentals of Engineering Exam which typically has a passing rate of less than 80%. From this point the statistics continue to spiral downward leaving us at a final percentage of about 20% who actually receive their PE license.

The guidelines and requirements in the modern era of engineering prove reliable when promoting public safety and welfare. Not only do the laws set in place never fail, they continue to grow safer as newer technology is created and used. Modern engineers have proved themselves worthy, holding the lowest failure rate ever recorded in history. Structural engineering has become a much mastered art form due to the many safe and consistently employed methods existing in the new century. It is easy to see that "Engineers are uniquely suited to contribute to the solution rather than the problem" (Burgess 1404). Engineering and the writing that is associated with it is a beautiful and necessary art that lets us sustain life through the use of science.

Works Cited

Blom, Andreas, and Hiroshi Saeki. "Employability and Skill Sets of Newly Graduated Engineers in India: A Study." *IUP Journal of Soft Skills*, vol. 6, no. 4, Dec. 2012, pp. 7–50. *EBSCOhost*, ezproxy.library.astate.edu/login?url=http://search.ebscohost.com/login.aspx?direct=true&db=bsh&AN=85170845&site=ehost-live

Burgess, Richard, et al. "Engineering Ethics: Looking Back, Looking Forward." *Science & Engineering Ethics*, vol. 19, no. 3, Sept. 2013, pp. 1395–1404. *EBSCOhost*, doi:10.1007/s11948-012-9374-7

French, Earl B. "The Organization Scientist: Myth or Reality." *Academy of Management Journal*, vol. 10, no. 3, Sept. 1967, pp. 269–273. *EBSCOhost*, doi:10.2307/255285

Hesse, Alex A., et al. "Approach-Span Failure of the Hoan Bridge as a Case Study for Engineering Students and Practicing Engineers." *Journal of Performance of Constructed Facilities*, vol. 28, no. 2, April 2014, pp. 341–348. *EBSCOhost*, ezproxy.library.astate.edu/login?url=http://search.ebscohost.com/login.aspx?direct=true&db=eoah&AN=32405556&site=ehost-live

Van Biesen, Leo Pierre, et al. "Engineering Skills Education: The Bachelor of Engineering Programme of the 'Vrije Universiteit Brussel' as a Case Study." *European Journal of Engineering Education*, vol. 34, no. 3, June 2009, pp. 217–228. EBSCOhost, doi:10.1080/03043790902721496

Sample Student Writing

Seth Price

Seth Price is a senior from Leachville, AR. He is an English B.S.E. student, with a minor in Writing Studies. In school, Seth always enjoyed writing, which is what led him towards the English Education degree. When Seth graduates, he wants to teach and coach football at the high school level. He has loved the game of football since the age of seven, and he spends much of his free time studying the game.

His favorite thing to write about is football, specifically in-depth strategy reports and analysis. He spent two semesters writing for The Herald, *the Arkansas State student newspaper, including one as the Sports Editor. After his time at* The Herald, *Seth served as a contributing writer for FOX Sports Knoxville. He also wrote and published a book, titled* Fast and Furious: Butch Jones and the Tennessee Volunteers' Offense, *which is a detailed analysis of Coach Jones' offensive philosophy.*

This particular assignment was written for Dr. Kristi Costello's Advanced Composition course. The piece was written in one sitting, followed by careful review. After a peer-review editing session, Seth submitted the essay to Dr. Costello. After getting the essay back, Seth met with Dr. Costello and revised the essay further.

Seth would advise other writers to never stop revising. Writers should seek the input of peers, professors, etc...and be willing to listen to their advice. No paper is ever perfect. There is always room for enhancement. Always edit what you write rigorously. Relentlessly pursue continuous improvement in your writing.

The Assignment: Op-Ed

A genre originally published opposite the editorial page in newspapers, op-eds are short, journalistic, argument-driven pieces commonly found in newspapers and online publications. Op-eds can focus on almost anything: Cultural, political, social, humanitarian, educational, or financial issues; particular people, places, or events; or even another op-ed. While informative, an op-ed's main purpose is to persuade the reader to see the issue, event, person, or place as the writer does. In fact, some op-eds go a step further and, in addition to adding to the readers' previous understanding of the issue, also ask for the readers to take action, such as writing a congresswoman a letter or boycotting a restaurant because of its discriminatory practices.

For this particular op-ed assignment, Seth and his classmates were asked to write an op-ed on any issue related to education, literacy, or language that would be of interest to the Arkansas State University community. They were also reminded to avoid logical fallacies and not to simply take an "either/or" argument, but rather concentrate on nuances of the issue that may have been missed or underdeveloped in previous sources or discussions. In other words, powerful op-eds say something new rather than rehashing the same tired arguments.

As you read, consider the ways that Seth brings in other viewpoints and adds to them with his own nuanced position. Note, also, the way he includes the sources of those viewpoints: Though he has a standard MLA Works Cited page, in the text of his essay he has no parenthetical citations. Instead, in the signal phrase before the quote, he often names the author and the book or newspaper in which it was published. Where he doesn't name the source directly, he cites it with a hyperlink. This citation style is common in online op-eds; most newspapers don't include parenthetical citations. As a writer for The Herald, Seth learned how journalists usually treat their sources.

What Do Standardized Tests Accomplish?

Seth Price

Op-Ed:
Written in Kristi Costello's Advanced Composition Class

. . . .

For as long as I can remember, standardized tests have been the way that schools measure how students learn. Students are tested yearly until they reach the early high school years. Then, all attention must be turned to the Benchmark, ACT and/or SAT, which are required to graduate and gain admittance into most colleges and universities. These tests have long been regarded as the best way to determine student achievement. Except...they aren't. Standardized tests do a poor job of measuring student achievement and fail to measure the effectiveness of a teacher.

One of the reasons standardized tests are not effective is that they fail to measure many of the attributes found in successful students. Sure, it's great to understand math, but what does it matter if you have no critical thinking skills? Understanding grammar is important, but so is having enthusiasm for your work. All students should have basic knowledge of science, but we should also be looking for creativity. These are just some of the traits that standardized tests do not even attempt to measure. In his book, *Education Hell: Rhetoric vs. Reality*, Gerald Bracey lists critical thinking, enthusiasm, and creativity among eighteen other important attributes that standardized tests make no effort to evaluate.

That's not to say the basic skills standardized tests evaluate, such as math, grammar, and reading, are not important—they are. But there is so much more required to be successful in this world, and to evaluate someone solely based on such a simple test is absurd. In fact, it may be hurting

students more than it helps them. When test makers ignore attributes they can't easily evaluate, students are encouraged to think superficially,[1] looking for the quick and easy answer. Students are led to believe that there is only one correct answer to a given question. Often those who score the best on standardized tests simply excel at memorizing facts, and the best score goes to the one who does extremely well at guessing the correct multiple choice answer. Standardized testing forces students to focus only on the simple and obvious answers, rather than critical and creative thinking. This is certainly not a habit we want to impress upon our children.

Successful students are those who are habitually involved in learning. It's easy to open up a textbook, follow the directions, and solve an algebra problem, but if you can't take the skills you learn and use them in the real world, have you really learned? In an article from *The Washington Post,* Marion Brady made the case that standardized tests do nothing to test "involved" learning skills. Being involved with the learning process by examining real plants outside the school or using an algebraic equation to measure the school's flagpole is a better way to learn than simply listening to a lecture.

Once the student becomes involved with the learning process, he or she will be able to maximize learning. However, with the rise of standardized tests, more and more focus is being placed on teaching students how to fill in a bubble and score positively on a test. Standardized tests have become far too important. Teachers need their students to score well so they can get the raise they desire and so their school can "make the grade" when it comes to achieving the quota of desirable scores set by education standards on Capitol Hill. Quite often, the priority shifts away from learning to simply beating the test, which means that teachers tend to "teach the test" rather than truly educating their students.

Because testing has become the focus in education, rote drill and test practice are more valued than application and creativity. This cookie-cutter concept of education, where each student is only measured by how many correct bubbles are filled in at the end of an allotted period of time, has resulted in standardized testing dictating curriculum. To produce high scores, educators must often exclude subject matter not included on standard tests. Classroom time is often devoted to teaching students test taking skills, even the best way to guess an answer, instead of the curriculum. Testing should not influence what is taught. In "Educational Leadership:

---

1 Price here cites in a hyperlink, as is common in online op-eds. This link points to the source by "Harris, Phillip, Joan Harris, and Bruce M. Smith," as cited in his Works Cited list.

Using Standards and Assessments: Why Standardized Tests Don't Measure Educational Quality," W. James Popham, Emeritus Professor in the UCLA Graduate School of Education and Information Studies, writes that using standardized tests to evaluate the quality of an educator is like "measuring temperature with a tablespoon." Just like a tablespoon was never designed to measure temperature, Popham states that standardized tests do a poor job of evaluating the effectiveness of a teacher, because that was not the purpose for which they were designed.

Despite their frequent and consistent use, standardized tests are also not a reliable way to grade student performance. A study published by the Brookings Institution and referenced in ProCon.org's analysis, "Standardized Tests," found that 50–80% of year-over-year test score improvements were "caused by fluctuations that had nothing to do with long-term changes in learning." Improvements students make from year to year have more to do with the randomness of the test than the education of the student. The same article discussed a report by the National Research Council which confirmed there is no evidence that standardized tests positively impact students at all. The report reads, "Despite using them for several decades, policymakers and educators do not yet know how to use test-based incentives to consistently generate positive effects on achievement and to improve education."

As a whole, standardized tests utterly fail to do the one thing they are supposed to do: measure student achievement. And this is not something to be taken lightly. With thousands of dollars in scholarships on the table, I, a current college student, fully understand the ramifications of these tests. But, if they cannot effectively evaluate a student's achievement, what purpose do standardized tests serve in their current form? Standardized testing can be useful only if it is used as one part of evaluation. However, in its present state, standardized tests cannot continue to be the main measure our nation uses to determine a successful student. As Dr. Diane Ravitch,[2] former U.S. Assistant Secretary of Education said in a speech quoted by *The Observer,* "Sometimes, the most brilliant and intelligent minds do not shine in standardized tests because they do not have standardized minds."

---

2 Here, Price is not citing the source of the quote but rather linking to Diane Ravitch's personal website (http://dianeravitch.com/), presumably to give interested readers more information about her.

Works Cited

Bracey, Gerald W. *Education Hell: Rhetoric vs. Reality.* Educational Research Service, 2009.

Brady, Marion. "What Do Standardized Tests Actually Test?" *Washington Post*, edited by Valerie Strauss, 1 Aug. 2014, www.washingtonpost. com/news/answer-sheet/wp/2014/08/01/what-do-standardized-tests-actually-test/?utm_term=.b3dafd536094. Accessed 2 Mar. 2016.

Harris, Phillip, Joan Harris, and Bruce M. Smith. "Standardized Tests Do Not Effectively Measure Student Achievement." *Opposing Viewpoints in Context.com*, 2012. *Galegroup*, ic.galegroup.com/ic/ovic/ ViewpointsDetailsPage/DocumentToolsPortletWindow?displayGrou pName=Viewpoints&jsid=80992fdc407e6f7147bbcf31f65c8332&actio n=2&catId=&documentId=GALE%7CEJ3010478218&u=uni_rodit&zi d=d6e7b4e81fc7b5eb428217a9cb8f362b. Accessed 2 Mar. 2016.

Hout, Michael, and Stuart W. Elliott, eds. *Incentives and Test-Based Accountability in Education.* Rep. National Research Council, 26 May 2011. *Proquest*, ebookcentral.proquest.com/lib/astate-ebooks/detail. action?docID=3378909. Accessed 4 Mar. 2016.

Neufeld, Jennifer. "Parents Band Together to End a 'Test-Obsessed System'." *Observer*, 23 Jan. 2015. *Observer*, observer.com/2015/01/parents-band-together-to-end-a-test-obsessed-system/. Accessed 17 Apr. 2016.

Popham, James, W. "Educational Leadership: Using Standards and Assessments: Why Standardized Tests Don't Measure Educational Quality." *Using Standards and Assessments*, vol 56, no. 6, 1999, www. ascd.org/publications/educational-leadership/mar99/vol56/num06/ Why-Standardized-Tests-Don't-Measure-Educational-Quality.aspx. Accessed 2 Mar. 2016.

"Standardized Tests." *ProConorg Headlines*, 3 Apr. 2015, standardizedtests. procon.org/. Accessed 2 Mar. 2016.

GARRET HARLOW

Garret Harlow, a senior agriculture business major, is from Memphis, Tennessee, but his frequent visits to Arkansas throughout his entire life make Arkansas like a second home. In his free time, he enjoys watching mixed martial arts, movies, reading, and spending time with his family and dogs during his visits home.

Garret's passion for writing emerged after taking a composition course with Dr. Kristi's Costello during his freshman year. He gives credit to Dr. Costello for showing him how to maximize his composition skills to be the best writer he could be, and explains, "She made writing essays fun. Writing was always a dread before having Dr. Costello." Garret says that he still uses these skills with every paper he has written during his academic career.

According to Garret, writing about subjects that you are passionate about is key to producing a solid, well written paper: "It is always fun to write about topics you have a passion for. It won't even feel like work if you have a passion for your writing."

THE ASSIGNMENT: RESEARCHED ARGUMENT

Much of the scholarship you read in your courses or in the journals most popular in your field are researched arguments. An effective researched argument examines a range of credible sources, including other scholarly articles, and discusses a range of perspectives on a contemporary issue being debated in academic disciplines.

For this assignment, students were asked to begin by conducting research on an academic topic of interest to them, preferably in their major. I encouraged them to critically read and compile sources and then consider where their voices, perspectives, and arguments fit into the existing conversation. Unlike a research report or paper (in which the sole aim is to inform), a researched argument asks writers to acknowledge, interpret, and analyze the current research, information, and perspectives on an issue with an eye toward ultimately contributing to this discussion with a unique insight, argument, or perspective.

Agriculture: Saving Civilization

Garret Harlow

Researched Argument:
Written in Kristi Costello's Composition II Class
· ·

Sample Student Writing

We live in an age when agriculture is crucial to our survival. Whether it is going to the grocery store to stock up the fridge and pantry or going to your favorite restaurant, agriculture is all around us, and our planet cannot be fed without it. Countries around the world depend on the United States to export crops to feed their people, and without these crops, their people will ultimately starve. Agriculture is the key to stalling worldwide hunger, and this solution is undercut by the lack of knowledge we have concerning the momentous effects agriculture has on our society. Until we begin proactively acknowledging the importance agriculture has in our society and take action accordingly, we, as a society, are destined to continue the destructive cycle of world hunger. There are many ways to cease world hunger, but the most productive and effective method is an emphasis on immense food production in the agricultural sector. By showing the benefits of agriculture, I will demonstrate to readers that, though we may not be able to completely end world hunger, we can start taking the appropriate steps to do so one day. In this paper, I will discuss agriculture's past and how it got to where it is today, and I will argue that America, the "Mother Country," has the technology and resources to start ending world hunger.

Before we examine the importance of agriculture in our world today, it is important to understand the history of agriculture. Though the true origin of agriculture remains unknown because the transition from hunter-gatherer societies began thousands years before the practice of writing, scholars like Bill Gammage believe the type of agriculture involving domestication of plants and animals was first developed around 10,000 B.C., as stated in his book *The Biggest Estate on Earth*. Besides this, there is an abundance of theories on the origins of agriculture. Most have been debunked by modern data, but the one most accepted among scholars is the theory that agriculture is a co-evolutionary adaptation of plants and humans, as David Rindos states in his book *The Origins of Agriculture: An Evolutionary Perspective*.

The first known agricultural practice was used by hunter-gatherers across Southwest Asia and North Africa. These hunter-gatherers would spend nearly all their time focusing on food. Emmer wheat and einkorn wheat were among the first crops to be grown, often referred to as the"founder crops." The crops that followed emmer and einkorn wheat were hulled barley, peas, lentils, bitter vetch, chick peas, and flax. These

crops were grown wild and not domesticated until about 3,000 years later. Professor Snell states in his book *Annals of the Labouring Poor, Social Change, and Agrarian England 1660–1900,* that between the 16th century and 19th century, Great Britain experienced an overwhelmingly massive increase in agricultural activity and net output. Unheard of agricultural practices began emerging, such as selective breeding, enclosure, four-field crop rotation, and mechanization. These practices propelled population growth and freed a large percentage of the workforce, which helped drive the Industrial Revolution. By the time the 19th century arrived, agricultural practices had improved drastically, and the yield per land unit was much more than those seen during the Middle Ages and before. The Agricultural Revolution proved to be a pivotal point in history. Agricultural production was taking off at rapid rates due to the machinery the farmers could utilize. The Industrial Revolution provided advanced knowledge in chemistry and science that helped produce fertilizers that farmers could use at their disposal. As stated by Jules Janick in her book *Agricultural Scientific Revolution: Mechanical,* there were many profound and revolutionary inventions such as the seed drill and threshing machine that, by the 20th century, increased agricultural production expeditiously, and by 1940, we had entered the Green Revolution. The Green Revolution lasted until the late 1970s and is said to have saved over one billion people from starvation. Agriculture helped pave the way for us, and without it, the human race would not be where it is at today. And now, agriculture is at its peak, with our unfathomable amount of technology. These facts help further prove the importance of agriculture for the survival of our people.

Without a doubt, the impact of agriculture on our food supply is momentous, and without our farms, we will ultimately starve. Most people go about their everyday lives without noticing the importance of our nation's farm sector. This may be because we take agriculture for granted, or it may be a lack of knowledge about farming. But the fact remains that without farms, there is no food. Every fast food chain, restaurant, and grocery store must get their product from a food distributor, which, in turn, gets its products from our farms. So it all starts at the farm. Eric Schlosser says in *Fast Food Nation,* "McDonald's is the nation's largest purchaser of beef, and like the rest of the world, McDonald's is dependent on these farmers producing healthy livestock and crops, because without them, the restaurant has no business, and we have no Big Macs to eat" (136).

The impact of U.S. agriculture goes far beyond domestic, though. Lester Brown, author of *Full Planet, Empty Plates* and the head of the U.S. Department of Agriculture's International Agricultural Development Service, gives straightforward and practical advice on how we should start saving the planet. In *Full Planet, Empty Plates,* he states "The United States is the world's leading producer and exporter of corn" (xi). Countries from all over the world depend on the United States for their supply of corn. Some people may not acknowledge the magnitude of this fact, but if our farmers decide to not work this year, it will almost guarantee the hunger of millions across the world. The amount of corn produced is also important because if not enough is produced, the price will rise, and some poorer countries will not be able to purchase the crop, guaranteeing the hunger of millions. Brown declares in *Full Planet, Empty Plates*, "The world is in transition from an era of food abundance to one of scarcity" (3). The momentous impact of the field of agriculture is significant because of the level of food production it creates and the people it feeds.

Our nation's agriculture department offers an abundance of support for increased agricultural production, such as jobs and eco-friendly farming, but the most important factor of increased production is the impact it can have on world hunger. Solutions to the world hunger problem may include population control and food rationing, but the most efficient and least intrusive method of ending world hunger is food production. Our planet is growing in population at an overwhelming speed, and our farms are going to be responsible for keeping these people fed. Brown says in *Full Planet, Empty Plates*, "On the demand side of the food equation, the world's population is increasing by nearly 80 million people a year. There will be 219,000 people at the dinner table tonight who were not there last night, many of them with empty plates. Tomorrow night there will be another 219,000 people" (9). With this steady population increase, we need more farms producing more food every day. Brown goes on to state, "In a hungry world, it is children who suffer the most. Rising food prices are leaving millions of children dangerously hungry. Some are too weak to walk to school. Many are so nutritionally deprived that they are physically and mentally stunted" (8). Most poor countries depend on America for their food supply. Families in countries like Peru, Nigeria, and those among the poorest class in India sometimes go days without food because they cannot afford it. If we produce more crops, prices will drop, and countries such as these will be able to purchase more food for their people. We should not stop people from reproducing, but we can be proactive and make plans for how we are going to feed our planet. Agriculture is the key to ending world hunger because of the mass food production it can create.

Agriculture is a crucial factor in ending worldwide hunger. Yet, some readers may challenge my view by insisting food rationing is ultimately the key to ending world hunger. Our nation possesses the necessary resources to inexpensively create gargantuan amounts of food to feed our world and put an end to world hunger, but much of the food we produce is currently wasted. Proponents of food rationing are right to argue that this waste of food does not help world hunger. But they exaggerate when they claim that food rationing is the most effective step to ending world hunger. When we

start emphasizing the importance of our farms, we will start taking appropriate steps to terminate the hunger of millions around the globe. While wasting large amounts of food does not help the situation, ultimately our farms are the key to ending world hunger.

Of course, many will disagree that agriculture can produce enough food to feed humanity on the grounds that our population is increasing at such rapid rates that it is impossible to produce food as quickly as we are producing people. These skeptics will insist that population control is the most effective method of filling hungry stomachs across the globe. Even Brown states in the book *Full Planet, Empty Plates*, "One of the consequences of this explosive growth in human numbers is that human demands have outrun the carrying capacity of the economy's natural support systems—its forests, fisheries, grasslands, aquifers, and soils" (15). These proponents of population control believe that if we adequately teach people the proper ways to avoid pregnancy, we will stall the rapid population increase and thus prevent the starvation of millions. These skeptics have reason to believe population control can affect global hunger more than we may originally notice. According to Brown, "Continuous population growth eventually leads to over plowing—the breaking of ground that is highly erodible and should not be plowed at all" (18). He goes on to state "The good news is that 44 countries, including nearly all those in both Western and Eastern Europe, have reached population stability as a result of gradual fertility decline over the last several generations" (50). Brown gives brilliant advice to proponents of population control by stating, "If your major concern is population growth, join one of the internationally oriented groups and lobby to fill the family planning gap" (123). While it is true that teaching people effective ways to control reproduction is important, the most effective method of ending world

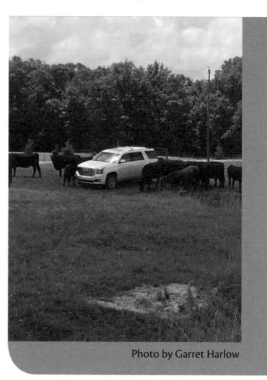

Photo by Garret Harlow

hunger would be emphasizing the momentous effect our farms can have on the millions who are starving if they are used efficiently. The most logical and attainable solution to world hunger is increased food production.

In summary, I believe the momentous benefits of increased agricultural production can save our planet. We need to acknowledge these benefits and start making a difference in our world by beginning to end world hunger, and this starts with our farms, plain and simple. Brown says, "We can prevent a breakdown of the food system, but it will require a huge political effort undertaken on many fronts and with a fierce sense of urgency" (123). I agree with this, and because we have the appropriate resources, it is time we act with the aforementioned urgency and put an end to foodless days for families both domestically and globally. I believe that Brown says it best: "We all have a stake in the future of civilization. Many of us have children. Some of us have grandchildren. We know what we have to do. It is up to you and me to do it. Saving civilization is not a spectator sport" (123).

Works Cited

Brown, Lester. *Full Planet, Empty Plates: The New Geopolitics of Food Scarcity.* W.W. Norton & Company, 2012.

Gammage, Bill. *The Biggest Estate on Earth: How Aborigines Made Australia.* Allin & Unwin, 2012.

Gunderson, Ralph, and Ospina Enrique. *The Structure of Arkansas Agriculture: A Taxonomy.* Winrock International Institute for Agricultural Development, 1986.

Heiser, Charles B. *Seed to Civilization: The Story of Food.* Harvard UP, 1990.

Janick, Jules. *Agricultural Scientific Revolution: Mechanical.* Purdue U, 2013.

Rindos, David. *The Origins of Agriculture: An Evolutionary Perspective.* Academic Press, 1987.

Schlosser, Eric. "On the Range." *Fast Food Nation: The Dark Side of the All-American Meal,* Houghton Mifflin Company, 2001. Perennial, an Imprint of Harper Collins, 2002.

Snell, K.D.M. *Annals of the Labouring, Social Change, and Agrarian England 1660–1900.* Cambridge U, 1985.

Sample Student Writing

NATHAN WALTERS

Nathan Walters is a native of Blytheville, Arkansas, and lived there until the age of three years old. Since that time, he has called the Bono and Jonesboro communities home. The entirety of his education took place at Westside Consolidated School District, home of the Warriors. He became an alumnus of his alma mater in 2014.

Walters's years at Westside stimulated his appreciation for writing. Assignments became opportunities to argue his viewpoints and express his values. Even though he is not pursuing a career in English or creative media, Walters believes that "writing is still crucial to my career path in the field of medicine. As I pursue a bachelor's degree in Biology with an emphasis in pre-professional studies and a minor in Spanish, writing is not foreign to me. As an aspiring medical doctor, scientific writing will remain a part of my future."

THE ASSIGNMENT: ARGUMENTATIVE ESSAY

An argumentative essay will usually respond directly to an issue that can vary in cultural or personal significance or importance to the author or reader. These papers can cover anything from local or national politics, to views on pop culture, or an issue that is currently in public discussion. It is important that the author take a specific, clear stand on the issue and make his or her views stronger by supporting them with researched evidence. Research in support of the thesis or argument only helps strengthen the validity and intensity of the author's view.

These papers are often brief, but they often require the author to go in search of evidence to support his or her views. This use of outside sources and research should strengthen and enhance the author's position. Authors should also investigate and discuss the views which oppose his or her argument, as this will bring clarity and a well-roundedness to the paper that allows the reader to judge the strength of the author's position in regards to the factual and practical aspects of the issue. In regards to this particular essay, the student was required to use effective transitions to ensure that his pattern of thoughts flows logically and is clear to readers.

Author photo by Roy Tanksley

Will You Settle for the Norm?

Nathan Walters

Argument Essay:
Written in Helen Duclos's Composition II Class

. . . .

Sample Student Writing

Any native of the South could easily sketch an elaborate scene of what most street corners in the region resemble. Aside from the typical asphalt roads, street lights, and concrete sidewalks, the other common factors are churches, banks, and restaurants. The vast majority of the restaurants provide a menu littered with fast food items. When did our society settle for the garbage that the fast food industry offers us?

Because of our extremely fast-paced society, many Americans buy into the idea that they are far too busy to prepare a home-cooked meal. The fast food industry is a controversial issue today, due to the exponential rise of obesity. One side of the debate places the United States' government in the hot seat, but the other side of the issue highlights the ultimate demand for personal responsibility of each American citizen. One aspect of life that hasn't changed over the years is time. There are still sixty minutes in an hour, twenty-four hours in a day, and roughly three hundred sixty-five days in one year. If Americans wish to combat the enslavement of obesity, then we must bite the bullet and independently assume personal responsibility for our health.

Since obesity's climb to fame as a national health epidemic, countless government anti-obesity initiatives have attempted to introduce a new solution or combat the issue. Just to name a few measures mentioned in "What You Eat Is Your Business," Radley Balko alludes to the fact that policy makers have introduced policies prohibiting junk food in school vending machines, demanding labels on food packages and menus, and federal funding for new bike trails and sidewalks (395–396). In the article "Remarks to the NAACP," Michelle Obama introduces the "Let's Move" initiative. It is designed to alter the lives of our children, by informing parents on how to make healthy decisions, introducing healthier foods in schools, encouraging an active lifestyle, and providing fresh, affordable food within American communities (425–427). Despite the fact that becoming a more informed public and having access to additional avenues for exercise improves health, the American society's perception of government initiatives is clouded. Once citizens are sold on the thought that everything the government introduces is a blessing for their well-being, sly policies can gain momentum with little resistance. For example, Balko later states, "Senator Joe Lieberman and Oakland Mayor Jerry Brown, among others, have called

for a 'fat tax' on high-calorie foods" (395–396). This proposed deterrent, as well as regulations prohibiting junk food in school vending machines, are simply infringements upon the rights of every American citizen to freely eat foods of their choosing. Allowing the government to be the hand that feeds your starving, deprived mouth is a major step toward socialism.

A few people will entertain the idea that the government should be the magician who swoops in and turns all of the chaos into beds of roses or fields of innocent, white bunny rabbits. But unless everyone in America is willing to relinquish all thought processes and simply become computer programed robots, as Aldous Huxley demonstrates in *Brave New World*, then we must take a stand and accept personal responsibility for our actions. Even though most people will try to deny any correlation between their lifestyle choices and that of their parents, the truth of the matter shines through. Our actions, eating habits, diction, and other lifestyle choices are greatly influenced by our parents and other individuals who invest their time in us.

With that being said, parents cannot continue to drop the ball. They must step up to the plate and teach their children about healthy eating practices. Just as children are taught to wipe their rear ends and wash their hands in order to practice good hygiene, they must receive instruction, practiced and demonstrated within the home, on how to prepare healthy meals. Wil Haygood alludes that overeating can be directly related to how a child is raised, in "Kentucky Town Illustrates National Obesity Crisis." Haygood mentions that cultural feelings toward food have shaped the way in which we consume. Due to the immense amount of financial hardships felt by the majority of the Unites States' citizens, a wasteful eater must be conditioned. In other words, it's common for an American household to adopt the "clean your plate" rule (Haygood 411). Although it is important to teach children the importance of not wasting food and other resources, it can become hazardous to their health to continually eat. If you only feed a baby until he or she loses the desire to drink from the bottle, why force feed a child beyond their desire to eat the food on his or her plate? Parents could simply encourage children to eat what they have been served without offering any other alternatives until the next meal. Making a commitment to address the initial spark that progresses into an uncontrollable lifestyle of overeating is only one key aspect in the fight against obesity.

Accepting personal responsibility for every aspect of an individual's life is crucial if we wish to completely combat the enslavement that obesity has on our society, as a whole. The magnifying glass of scrutiny should fall upon parents and independent adults, instead of the government. The government insists on accepting the blame in order to create a dependency. This robs every American citizen of their independence. We have already

Sample Student Writing

seen this occur with government healthcare reform. It may sound great to provide for those who cannot afford medical insurance, but who is going to compensate for the average American's premium increase, in response? Leaving healthcare choices in the hands of the people would demand personal responsibility. The American society isn't incompetent; we simply choose to be lazy. A large majority of people who struggle to pay their bills, and survive in life, suffer because they are a poor manager of their priorities. Food, clothing, shelter, job security, and transportation should be the main concern. All other wants can be sought after with the remainder of one's income. Sadly, many individuals buy into materialism and live beyond one's means, in order to achieve acceptance from peers and contentment. For example, fresh foods could be bought instead of the latest smartphone or newest pair of jeans. Simply crying that healthy, fresh food is too expensive isn't acceptable. Nearly everything we purchase is overpriced. The average pair of jeans cost at least fifty dollars a pair. Another crutch that many people cling to is that there isn't enough time to complete all obligations and cook a healthy meal. Dedicate less time to entertainment, such as social media and television, and set aside a time frame for preparing a meal. A balanced set of priorities coupled with a sense of personal responsibility could cripple the obesity epidemic.

Works Cited

Balko, Radley. "What You Eat Is Your Business." *They Say/I Say: The Moves That Matter in Academic Writing: With Readings*, 3rd ed., edited by Gerald Graff, Cathy Birkenstein, and Russel Durst, W.W. Norton & Co., 2012, pp. 395–398.

Haygood, Wil. "Kentucky Town of Manchester Illustrates National Obesity Crisis." *They Say/I Say: The Moves That Matter in Academic Writing: With Readings*, 2nd ed., edited by Gerald Graff, Cathy Birkenstein, and Russel Durst, New York: W.W. Norton & Co., 2012, pp. 406–415.

Obama, Michelle. "Remarks to the NAACP National Convention." *They Say/I Say: The Moves That Matter in Academic Writing: With Readings*, 2nd ed., edited by Gerald Graff, Cathy Birkenstein, and Russel Durst, New York: W.W. Norton & Co., 2012, pp. 417–433.

PATRICK TRIBBETT

Patrick Tribbett is a physics major with a mathematics and chemistry minor from Baltimore, Maryland. In his free time, he also enjoys spending time playing music and cooking.

Even though he spends far more time in a lab or with a chalkboard than in an English class, he believes quality writing is a necessary tool. Without a solid foundation from Composition I and II, effective communication, a prerequisite for success in any discipline, would be impossible.

THE ASSIGNMENT: POSITION PAPER

A position paper will often require the reader to take a position on a particular topic that is of importance in society. After reading about and discussing a particular issue, the author should state and defend a position on that issue as well as to illustrate how his or her opinion relates to similar or opposing opinions about the same issue. These papers can cover anything that piques the author's interest, from local or national politics, to views on pop culture, or an issue that is currently popular in public discussion. When writing, the author must present a specific and clear thesis, one that takes a stand on the issue. In this assignment, there is no room for "riding the fence."

In a position paper, there is an emphasis on the use of logic to support the author's personal position. Using logos (along with other rhetorical appeals) makes the author seem well-organized and prepared to defend his or her position instead of someone who is in the middle of a rant or tirade. Additionally, the author should validate his or her views by supporting them with researched evidence. Research in support of the author's position (or thesis) only helps strengthen the validity and intensity of the author's view in the minds of the readers. Authors should always investigate and discuss the viewpoint(s) that opposes his or her own position, as this will bring clarity and a sense of well-roundedness to the paper that allows the reader to judge the strength of the author's position in regards to the factual and practical aspects of the issue.

Monsters in the Media

Patrick Tribbett

Position Paper:
Written in Kerri Bennett's Composition II Class

· ·

Sample Student Writing

· ·

Note: This is the polished draft of Tribbett's essay. It has been revised by the author after receiving annotations from the instructor. The annotated version is available in Chapter 6 of the book.

· ·

Modern monsters tend to display deviant behavioral or physical characteristics, a definition that the media uses to vilify groups of people with unusual traditions or traits. This categorization incites panic and distrust among the general population, constructing a consensus that these minorities are monstrous. Throughout its brief history, mass media identifies 'others' and over-exemplifies negative qualities in an attempt to skew an audience's perception of a group of individuals; several examples include immigrants of religious minorities and medical patients, most commonly HIV and mental health patients.

During an influx of the immigration of religious minorities, the mass media affirms differences between the immigrants and the general population in order to divide the people into the normal and the others. By describing the difference as "arbitrary and potentially free-floating, mutable rather than essential [and that] the monster threatens to destroy not just individual members of society, but the very cultural apparatus through which individuality is constituted and allowed," mass media can completely vilify and dehumanize religious immigrants (Cohen 20). This type of propaganda direly affected Jewish immigrants in the early 20th century and is now creating problems for Syrian refugees in the United States.

Gothic novelists during the early 20th century portray certain monsters with anti-Semitic generalizations. Bram Stoker's original Dracula, for example, exemplifies different offensive Jewish stereotypes such as a "high bridge of the thin nose and peculiarly arched nostrils," a "heavy moustache, [that] was fixed and rather cruel-looking," and "the general effect of extraordinary pallor" (113). Furthermore, the gothic vampire's monstrous obsessions include blood and money, which are closely associated with anti-Semitic ideology (Halberstam 131). The media, in fear for their traditions,

vilified these characteristics to splice the immigrants out of the general population. This exact discrimination occurs in the United States today against the Muslim immigrants from Syria. According to researchers Erin Steuter and Deborah Wills, "newspaper headlines [are] influentially compressed narratives replicating and recycling key metaphors that systematically figure [Muslims] as animal, vermin, or metastatic disease" (152). Since the 9/11 terrorist attacks, the mass media indiscriminately vilifies all Muslims "as carriers of a religiously-specific pathology," because their traditions and rituals differ from those most common in the United States (Steuter and Wills 155). This dehumanization style of segregation causes entirely unnecessary fear and distrust among the American population.

Along with immigrants, medical patients, specifically HIV and mental health patients, also endure vilification from mass media. Sexual deviance is commonly represented in modern media as the other; vampirism, for example, portrays a sexually variant, sexual penetration through biting instead of traditional intercourse. Similarly, a sexually non-traditional couple in *American Horror Story: Hotel*, Elizabeth and Donavan, are portrayed as monsters, slitting the throats of their partners and savoring the blood. This othering also extends to HIV patients. In fact, "Western media provided a key site for the cultural production of HIV/AIDS as a disease of the 'other', making possible the idea that infection was linked to identities located outside the 'mainstream'; outside 'proper' heterosexuality...media coverage in the 1980s and 1990s was marked by the [demonization] of gay men" (Persson and Newman 632). In fear of the abandonment of heterosexuality, mass media vilifies nontraditional sexual orientation by displaying HIV patients as the result of nonconformity to the cultural norm.

In addition, medical patients diagnosed with mental health disorders received a similar discrimination from the mass media. According to the Scottish Mental Health Working group, a majority of mass media content regarding mental health highlights five main categories associated with mental health and illness: "violence to others, harm to self, sympathetic coverage, criticism of accepted definition of mental illness, and 'comic' images" (Cutcliffe 316). The othering of mental health patients drastically contributes to the stigma felt by the patients. Many popular television series, such as *Criminal Minds*, *Bones*, and *CSI*, contain an extraordinary high amount of material linking mental health issues and violent crime. This over-exemplification of violence in the mental health community, a proportionally small subgroup, misrepresents the larger whole of the group, and leads to distrust among the rest of the population.

The mass media identifies groups of individuals that possess unusual characteristics or traditions, and overly displays their negative qualities to change the population's perception of them. This creates an unnecessary distrust and fear between the 'normal' and 'other' communities.

Works Cited

Cohen, Jeffrey J. "Monster Culture (Seven Theses)." *Monsters*, edited by Brandy B. Blake and L. Andrew Cooper, Fountainhead Press, 2012, pp. 11–33.

Cutcliffe, J. R. and B. Hannigan. "Mass Media, 'Monsters' and Mental Health Clients: The Need For Increased Lobbying." *Journal of Psychiatric and Mental Health Nursing*, vol. 8, 2001, pp. 315–321. *Academic Search Complete*, DOI: 10.1046/j.1365-2850.2001.00394.x

Halberstam, Judith. "Parasites and Perverts: an Introduction to Gothic Monstrosity." *Monsters*, edited by Brandy B. Blake and L. Andrew Cooper, Fountainhead Press, 2012, pp. 123–138.

Persson, Asha, and Christy Newman. "Making Monsters: Heterosexuality, Crime and Race in Recent Western Media Coverage of HIV." *Sociology of Health & Illness*, vol. 30, no. 4, 2008, pp. 632–646. *Academic Search Complete*, DOI: 10.1111/j.1467-9566.2008.01082.x

Steuter, Erin and Deborah Willis. "'The Vermin have struck again': dehumanizing the enemy in post 9/11 media representations." *Journal of Media, War & Conflict*, vol. 3, no. 2, 2010, pp. 152–167. *Communication & Mass Media Complete*, DOI: 10.1177/1750635210360082

Stoker, Bram. "Excerpts from Dracula." *Monsters*, edited by Brandy B. Blake and L. Andrew Cooper, Fountainhead Press, 2012, pp. 113–120.

Sample Student Writing

GABRIELLE RANNALS

Gabrielle Rannals was born in Jonesboro, AR and raised in Paragould, AR. She lives on a farm with her two dogs that she adores. Even though she resides almost an hour from the A-state campus, she commutes and arrives hours before her classes start. She says, "being ahead of my tasks and consistently being prepared is a huge part of my motivation and success with my academics." She believes it is important to stay true to yourself and to do the best in everything you do. She loves her family and she encourages others to creatively express themselves.

THE ASSIGNMENT: ARGUMENT IN AN INFOGRAPHIC

You may have heard that everything around you is a form of argument, but it is unlikely that you have ever tried to create one outside the familiar medium of the printed word. However, traditional textual arguments are only one of many ways authors can present their positions to their audiences. Using charts, graphs, and other images to display information, known as infographics, can also be effective means to convey desired messages.

By reading data with a critical eye and arranging it carefully, you can use scientific research to persuade your audience, perhaps even when the same group could not be easily swayed through the use of words alone. To this end, you will use rhetorical strategies to practice the art of visual argumentation. Your infographic must present data from a research report in a variety of charts and graphs. The title of your infographic should make a clear point that is supported with subheadings (which make subclaims), and you should demonstrate your point through the evidence in your graphs. Be sure to represent ten or more data points both literally and abstractly in those graphs, making sure they are arranged in an interesting way. Finally, cite the name of the research group responsible for the report you used to create your infographic along with a URL to the actual report you used.

Regarding citations, Gabrielle's instructor for the class, Elizabeth Chamberlain, notes that: This infographic is the only piece in this book without citations in MLA, APA, or Chicago style. When you compose in a genre outside the bounds of traditional academic essays, you'll look for models to understand how it works: How it begins. How it ends. How it looks. How it's organized. But you should also consider how its composers treat sources. Do they cite in the body of the piece, or only at the end? Do they include links? Titles? Names of creators? Do they follow any standard citation format, or does it vary?

*Most infographics cite sources, as Gabrielle Rannals has done, in a footnote at the bottom of the image. This infographic draws from just one source—but when an infographic has multiple sources, composers will sometimes distinguish among them in the body with symbols corresponding to footnotes (e.g., * vs † vs +).*

If your composition instructor assigns a digital composition (such as an infographic, a video, or an audio essay), you'll discuss how to cite appropriately in that genre. Though citation styles differ from genre to genre and field to field, they all have the same goal: To give credit where credit is due.

What Americans Lack in Scientific Knowledge

Gabrielle Rannals

Argument in an Infographic: Written in Elizabeth Chamberlain's Composition I Class

. . . .

Please see the infographic on the following page.

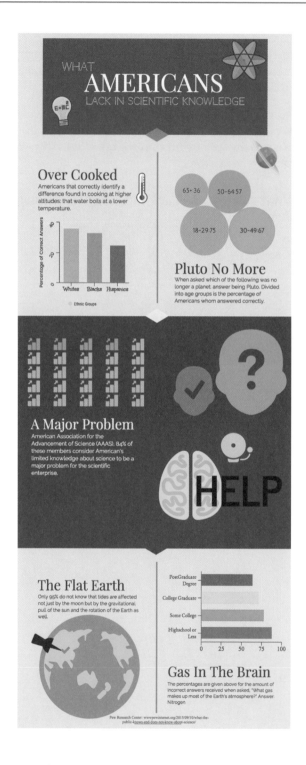

WHAT AMERICANS
LACK IN SCIENTIFIC KNOWLEDGE

$E=mc^2$

Over Cooked
Americans that correctly identify a difference found in cooking at higher altitudes: that water boils at a lower temperature.

Percentage of Correct Answers

Whites Blacks Hispanics

Ethnic Groups

65+·36   50-64·57

18-29·75   30-49·67

Pluto No More
When asked which of the following was no longer a planet answer being Pluto. Divided into age groups is the percentage of Americans whom answered correctly.

A Major Problem
American Association for the Advancement of Science (AAAS), 84% of these members consider American's limited knowledge about science to be a major problem for the scientific enterprise.

?
✓

HELP

The Flat Earth
Only 95% do not know that tides are affected not just by the moon but by the gravitational pull of the sun and the rotation of the Earth as well.

PostGraduate Degree

College Graduate

Some College

Highschool or Less

0   25   50   75   100

Gas In The Brain
The percentages are given above for the amount of incorrect answers received when asked, "What gas makes up most of the Earth's atmosphere?" Answer: Nitrogen

Pew Research Center: www.pewinternet.org/2015/09/10/what-the-public-knows-and-does-not-know-about-science/

Conclusion

We hope that these contextualized examples help you better prepare for the writing tasks asked of you in Composition II. As you can see, instructors in our program hope to be as transparent as possible, not only about our assignments, but also the goals we have for you as budding scholars and our methods of evaluating your performance to these goals. We design our assignments to speak clearly to our goal of preparing you for your discipline and we believe that the sample student essays we provide hold true to these goals. Don't hesitate to use this book, and the information contained within, to engage in meaningful class discussion, not only about the writing tasks you are assigned but also the pedagogical theories that drive them and the disciplinary awareness we aim to instill in you.

Introduction

This brief chapter contains a text created by a student along with comments on the text from the student's instructor. The assignment sheet for the project precedes the text, providing context for the assignment and its requirements. We've included the annotated student project for two reasons. First, the annotations offer an idea of how to provide constructive feedback to another writer (take note of how the instructor gives specific suggestions that the author can use to revise the paper). Second, the annotated essay will give you a sense of the sort of issues your instructors are focusing upon when creating comments for and evaluating your writing, making transparent the process instructors use to assess your work. To see the polished draft of this essay please refer to the sample essays we have provided in the preceding section of this book.

Patrick Tribbett

Patrick Tribbett is a physics major with a mathematics and chemistry minor from Baltimore, Maryland. In his free time, he also enjoys spending time playing music and cooking.

Even though he spends far more time in a lab or with a chalkboard than in an English class, he believes quality writing is a necessary tool. Without a solid foundation from Composition I and II, effective communication, a prerequisite for success in any discipline, would be impossible.

The Assignment: Position Paper

A position paper will often require the reader to take a position on a particular topic that is of importance in society. After reading about and discussing a particular issue, the author should state and defend a position on that issue as well as to illustrate how his or her opinion relates to similar or opposing opinions about the same issue. These papers can cover anything that piques the author's interest, from local or national politics, to views on pop culture, or an issue that is currently popular in public discussion. When writing, the author must present a specific and clear thesis, one that takes a stand on the issue. In this assignment, there is no room for "riding the fence."

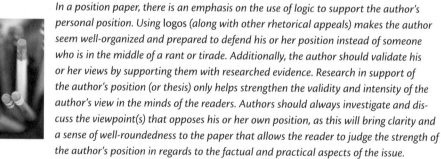

In a position paper, there is an emphasis on the use of logic to support the author's personal position. Using logos *(along with other rhetorical appeals) makes the author seem well-organized and prepared to defend his or her position instead of someone who is in the middle of a rant or tirade. Additionally, the author should validate his or her views by supporting them with researched evidence. Research in support of the author's position (or thesis) only helps strengthen the validity and intensity of the author's view in the minds of the readers. Authors should always investigate and discuss the viewpoint(s) that opposes his or her own position, as this will bring clarity and a sense of well-roundedness to the paper that allows the reader to judge the strength of the author's position in regards to the factual and practical aspects of the issue.*

Monsters in the Media

Patrick Tribbett

Position Paper:
Written in Kerri Bennett's Composition II Class

Note: This is the initial or rough draft of Tribbett's essay. It has been annotated by the instructor to show areas which need to be improved in the next draft as well as the particular strengths that make this essay a good example of a position paper.

Modern monsters tend to display deviant behavioral or physical characteristics, a definition that the media uses to vilify groups of people with unusual traditions or traits. This categorization incites panic and distrust among the general population, constructing a consensus that these minorities are monstrous. Throughout its brief history, mass media identifies 'others' and over-exemplifies negative qualities in attempt to skew an audience's perception of a group of individuals; several examples include immigrants of religious minorities and medical patients, most commonly HIV and mental health patients.

> This is a good thesis. It clearly states your opinion as well as previews what you will discuss in your essay.

> An article is missing here.

During an influx of the immigration of religious minorities, the mass media affirms differences between the immigrants and the general population in order to divide the people into the normal and the others. By describing the difference as "arbitrary and potentially free-floating, mutable rather than essential [and that] the monster threatens to destroy not just individual members of society, but the very cultural apparatus through which individuality is constituted and allowed," mass media can completely vilify and dehumanize religious immigrants (Cohen 20). This type of propaganda direly affected Jewish immigrants in the early 20th century and is now creating problems for Syrian refugees in the United States.

> I like the use of a concrete example here to show that the problems of the past continue into present day.

Annotated Student Essay

Gothic novelists during the early 20th century portray certain monsters with anti-Semitic generalizations. Bram Stoker's original Dracula, for example, exemplifies different offensive Jewish stereotypes such as a "high bridge of the thin nose and peculiarly arched nostrils," a "heavy moustache, [that] was fixed and rather cruel-looking," and "the general effect of extraordinary pallor" (113). Furthermore, the gothic vampire's monstrous obsessions include blood and money, which are closely associated with anti-Semitic ideology (Halberstam 131). These characteristics were used by the media, in fear for their traditions, to vilify the immigrants and splice them out of the general population. This exact discrimination occurs in the United States today against the Muslim immigrants from Syria. According to researchers Erin Steuter and Deborah Wills, "newspaper headlines [are] influentially compressed narratives replicating and recycling key metaphors that systematically figure [Muslims] as animal, vermin, or metastatic disease" (152). Since the 9/11 terrorist attacks, the mass media indiscriminately vilifies all Muslims "as carriers of a religiously-specific pathology," because their traditions and rituals differ from those most common in the United States (Steuter and Wills 155). This dehumanization style of segregation causes entirely unnecessary fear and distrust among the American population.

Along with immigrants, medical patients, specifically HIV and mental health patients, also endure vilification from mass media. Sexual deviance is commonly represented in modern media as the other: vampirism, for example, portrays a sexually variant, sexual penetration through biting instead of traditional intercourse. Moreover, a sexually non-tradition couple in *American Horror Story: Hotel*, Elizabeth and Donavan, are portrayed as monsters, slitting the throats of their partners and savoring the blood. This othering extends to HIV patients. In fact, "Western media provided a key site for the cultural production of HIV/AIDS as a disease of the 'other', making possible the idea that infection was linked to identities located outside the 'mainstream'; outside 'proper' heterosexuality... media coverage in the 1980s and 1990s was marked by the [demonization] of gay men" (Persson and Newman 632). In fear of the abandonment of heterosexuality, mass media

This is a nicely incorporated direct quotation that is used to support both the topic of the paragraph and the thesis.

Can you rephrase to use active voice here? I think your meaning would be clearer.

This is a nice transition from one topic to the next.

Change to "non-traditional."

Consider a paragraph break here.

vilifies nontraditional sexual orientation by displaying HIV patients as the result of nonconformity to the cultural norm. Medical patients diagnosed with mental health disorders received a similar discrimination from the mass media. According to the Scottish Mental Health Working group, a majority of mass media content regarding mental health highlights five main categories associated with mental health and illness: "violence to others, harm to self, sympathetic coverage, criticism of accepted definition of mental illness, and 'comic' images" (Cutcliffe 316). The othering of mental health patients drastically contributes to the stigma felt by the patients. Many popular television series, such as *Criminal Minds*, *Bones*, and *CSI*, contain an extraordinary high amount of material linking mental health issues and violent crime. This over-exemplification of violence in the mental health community, a proportionally small subgroup, misrepresents the larger whole of the group, and leads to distrust among the rest of the population.

Though brief, the conclusion hearkens back to your original thesis, neatly signaling an end to the argument.

The mass media identifies groups of individuals that possess unusual characteristics or traditions, and overly displays their negative qualities to change the population's perception of them. This creates an unnecessary distrust and fear between the 'normal' and 'other' communities.

Works Cited

Cohen, Jeffrey J. "Monster Culture (Seven Theses)." *Monsters,* edited by Brandy B. Blake and L. Andrew Cooper, Fountainhead Press, 2012, pp. 11–33.

Cutcliffe, J. R. and B. Hannigan. "Mass Media, 'Monsters' and Mental Health Clients: The Need For Increased Lobbying." *Journal of Psychiatric and Mental Health Nursing,* vol. 8, 2001, pp. 315–321. *Academic Search Complete,* DOI: 10.1046/j.1365-2850.2001.00394.x

Halberstam, Judith. "Parasites and Perverts: an Introduction to Gothic Monstrosity." *Monsters,* edited by Brandy B. Blake and L. Andrew Cooper, Fountainhead Press, 2012, pp. 123–138.

Persson, Asha, and Christy Newman. "Making Monsters: Heterosexuality, Crime and Race in Recent Western Media Coverage of HIV." *Sociology of Health & Illness,* vol. 30, no. 4, 2008, pp. 632–646. *Academic Search Complete,* DOI: 10.1111/j.1467-9566.2008.01082.x

Steuter, Erin and Deborah Willis. "'The Vermin have struck again': dehumanizing the enemy in post 9/11 media representations." *Journal of Media, War & Conflict,* vol. 3, no. 2, 2010, pp. 152–167. *Communication & Mass Media Complete,* DOI: 10.1177/1750635210360082

Stoker, Bram. "Excerpts from Dracula." *Monsters,* edited by Brandy B. Blake and L. Andrew Cooper, Fountainhead Press, 2012, pp. 113–120.

Sample Papers in MLA, Chicago, and APA Styles

Sample Papers in Different Styles

In this section we provide you with examples of argumentative papers in three different formatting and documentation styles, APA (American Psychological Association), MLA (Modern Language Association), and CMS (Chicago Manual of Style). The goal is not only to provide you with models for citation in the different styles, but also to demonstrate the rhetorical and stylistic conventions of each. As you read through the samples, take time to notice the nuances of each style. Ask yourself how the varied parenthetical citations affect your reading. How does the use of footnotes allow the author to present information? Why are dates used in parenthetical citations in APA, but not in MLA? How do the requirements of each style represent what the field values most? Keep in mind that the conventions of each style were decided on by a board of experts in the field who believe that the current models (i.e., APA 6, CMS 6, MLA 8) are the best ways for research in their disciplines to be presented to readers. As you become more familiar with documentation styles, ask yourself if you agree with their choices.

Amber Hatcher

Amber Hatcher is a sophomore at Arkansas State University from Trumann, AR. When she is not in class or working, she enjoys reading, writing, and spending time with her husband.

Ever since she was four years old, she knew that her purpose in life was to write. She loves writing, not only to escape this world herself, but to let others escape as well. A quote from the Harry Potter character, Albus Dumbledore best describes how she feels about writing: "Words are, in my not-so-humble opinion, our most inexhaustible source of magic."

The Assignment: Argumentative Essay

An argumentative essay is a formal piece in which the student demonstrates the ability to present a strong argument with attention to the rhetorical appeals, acknowledgement of and response to counterargument, and the ability to select, evaluate, and incorporate sources alongside original ideas.

This type of essay can cover anything from local or national politics, to views on pop culture, or issues currently in public discussion, but it also requires the author to go in search of evidence to support his or her views. This use of outside sources and research should strengthen and enhance the author's position. An author should also investigate and discuss the views which oppose his or her argument, as this will bring clarity and a well-roundedness to the paper that allows the reader to judge the strength of the author's thesis.

Sample Essay in MLA Style (8th Edition)

Amber Hatcher

Written for Geoffrey Clegg's Composition II Class

Hatcher 1

Amber Hatcher

Mr. Clegg

ENG 1013

November 12, 2014

Muggles and Mudbloods and Creatures, Oh My!

Racism in the Wizarding World

Racism has been a major problem in society for centuries. As a result, it has become a key theme in various works of literature, including the *Harry Potter* series. J.K. Rowling gives a clear insight into how racism has affected the world of humans by illustrating it through a world of magic. She divides the racism in the wizarding world into three major categories throughout the series.

The first category concerning racism in the *Harry Potter* series is the distinction between purebloods and non-purebloods. Lord Voldemort belonged to the Slytherin House while he attended Hogwarts School of Witchcraft and Wizardry. Out of all four houses (Gryffindor, Hufflepuff, Ravenclaw, and Slytherin), Slytherin housed several students who turned evil. The founder of the Slytherin House, Salazar Slytherin, only wanted pureblood students to attend Hogwarts. He did not think half-bloods or Muggle-borns were worthy enough to attend. He was outnumbered, how-ever, as the other founders disagreed. Salazar Slytherin then built the Chamber of Secrets, killing students who were not pureblood. The other founders quickly discovered it, closing the Chamber and banishing Salazar Slytherin from Hogwarts. Years later, Tom Riddle, Salazar Slytherin's heir, reopened the Chamber and continued his legacy.

   J.K. Rowling compares Lord Voldemort to Hitler. Both believed in racial purity, although they themselves were not what they believed to be pure. Hitler had Jewish blood, and Tom Riddle was a half-blood. Because of this, their killing people of their own blood "might have been an attempt to eliminate the part of himself he loathed" (Whited 3). She also says that the reopening of the Chamber "coincides with the opening of the Nazis' death chambers" (Whited 3). Racism transpired to the modern times of the wizarding world but not to the same extent, at first. Although the Chamber was once again reopened by Tom Riddle, racism dealt more with verbal abuse. This can be seen by Draco Malfoy's constant comments towards Hermione Granger, such as when he called her a "filthy little Mudblood" (*Chamber of Secrets* 112), which is a cruel name pureblood wizards use to describe Muggle-borns. It can also be seen by the portrait of Mrs. Black, Sirius' mother, who shouts obscenities like, "FILTHY HALF-BREEDS, BESMIRCHING THE HOUSE OF MY FATHERS" (*Order of the Phoenix* 179) and "MUDBLOODS! SCUM! CREATURES OF DIRT!" (*Order of the Phoenix* 180) whenever the Order of the Phoenix meets at Number Twelve, Grimmauld Place. However, after Dumbledore's death, Voldemort's followers, the Death Eaters, took over. The Ministry of Magic was going through drastic changes, including the addition of a new department called the "Muggle-Born Registration Commission." The proceedings to determine whether a witch or wizard was a Muggle-born were very much like the Salem Witch Trials. A witch or wizard would be accused of being a Muggle-born, even if they were half-bloods. At the hearing of Mary Cattermole, Yaxley, the new Minister of Magic, states, "The brats of Mudbloods do not stir our sympathies" (*Deathly Hallows* 259), and Dolores Umbridge tells her, "Wands only choose witches or wizards. You are not a witch" (*Deathly Hallows* 261). If any witch or wizard had Muggles in their family, they were registered as a Muggle-born.

The next manner of racism in the wizarding world is between wizards and magical creatures. There are several wizards who are kind to the magical beings (house-elves, werewolves, etc.), but there are others who treat them as though they are nothing. During the times of slavery in America, slaves were not viewed as equals. This is also the case for house-elves. Dobby, a house-elf, is a slave to the Malfoys. When Dobby arrives at the Dursley's, Harry suggests that Dobby sit down. Dobby bursts into to tears, stating, "Dobby has *never* been asked to sit down by a wizard—like an equal" (*Chamber of Secrets* 13). Also like the slaves, house-elves are beaten whenever they do something wrong. Dobby tells Harry, "Dobby is always having to punish himself for something...Sometimes they reminds me to do extra punishments" (*Chamber of Secrets* 14).

Some wizards did not like werewolves or giants. In *Prisoner of Azkaban*, the first werewolf in the series is introduced as the new Defense Against the Dark Arts professor, Remus Lupin. While talking to Harry in the Shrieking Shack, he tells him that "other parents weren't likely to want their children exposed to me" (*Prisoner of Azkaban* 353). He also tells Harry "I have been shunned all my adult life, unable to find paid work because of what I am" (*Prisoner of Azkaban* 356). Even though he stayed away from people during the one week a month when he turned into a werewolf and started taking the Wolfsbane Potion so he could still have his human thoughts, people still feared him. Dolores Umbridge is one of the more racist wizards concerning magical creatures, which is seen when she calls the centaurs "Filthy half-breeds!...Beasts! Uncontrolled animals!" (*Order of the Phoenix* 755). These magical creatures are part-human or have human characteristics, but because they are a different race than the majority of wizards, they are prejudiced against them.

The third and final type of racism in the *Harry Potter* series is between wizards and Muggles. Wizards know that Muggles exist, but "only a very

Sample Essay in MLA Style (8th Edition)

Hatcher 4

limited number of Muggles know about Wizards"[1] (Bertilsson 5). The ones that do typically consider them strange or fear them. The Dursleys are one of the groups of Muggles that hate wizards. This is why they ignore anything unusual and try to keep Harry from attending Hogwarts. Whenever they took him in, they "had hoped that if they kept Harry as downtrodden as possible, they would be able to squash the magic out of him" (*Prisoner of Azkaban* 2). Their attempts were unsuccessful, however. When Harry first received his acceptance letter into Hogwarts, Vernon tells Petunia, "I'm not having one in the house, Petunia! Didn't we swear when we took him in we'd stamp out this dangerous nonsense?" (*Sorcerer's Stone* 36). Harry cannot even say the word "magic" in their house without being yelled at. When Uncle Vernon tells Harry to give him a pan, Harry asks for the magic word. Uncle Vernon becomes angry, yelling "WHAT HAVE I TOLD YOU ABOUT SAYING THE 'M' WORD IN OUR HOUSE?" and "I WILL NOT TOLERATE MENTION OF YOUR ABNORMALITY UNDER THIS ROOF!" (*Chamber of Secrets* 2).

Some wizards, like Mr. Weasley, who works for the Misuse of Muggle Artifacts department in the Ministry of Magic, find Muggles fascinating. Other wizards, such as the Malfoys, look down upon Muggles and upon those wizards who think there is nothing wrong with Muggles. Lucius Malfoy looks pointedly at Hermione's parents after Mr. Weasley states, "We have a very different idea of what disgraces the name of wizard" (*Chamber of Secrets* 62). Then, while talking about Mr. Weasley, Pius Thicknesse says, "If you ask me, the blood traitors are as bad as the Mudbloods" (*Deathly Hallows* 247). This goes back to the concept of Slytherins only believing that purebloods should be allowed an education at Hogwarts.

The same problems that were seen in our world during the Holocaust and during the times of slavery are also seen in J.K. Rowling's *Harry Potter*

---

1 Notice that "Wizards" is capitalized in this instance because it is capitalized in the article (Ed.).

book series. Although Muggles and wizards are both human, and although non-purebloods and magical creatures share the same magical powers as wizards, they are looked down upon in the wizarding world. They are not seen as equals by many, even though they make up the majority of the population. J.K. Rowling reminds us that racism is still a problem today through her unforgettable world of characters.

However, some people suggest that J.K. Rowling is a racist herself. The main support for this claim is the fact that the majority of the characters in the *Harry Potter* series are white. According to a 2001 census of the United Kingdom, where the series takes place, "it puts the total of white people in the UK at 92.14%" (Adam). Harry would have graduated a few years before this, so it makes sense that white people form the bulk of the student body and staff. However, that is not the problem. The problem is that the characters who are of a different race are only minor characters. Take Dean Thomas and Angelina Johnson, for instance. They are both black students, but barely get any recognition. Angelina Johnson is only referred to when talking about Quidditch, the wizarding sport, and Dean is best known as his role as Ginny Weasley's boyfriend before she finally ends up with Harry.

Another character is Cho Chang. She first appears in *Harry Potter and the Goblet of Fire*, when Harry develops a crush on her. They are together briefly in the next book, *Harry Potter and the Order of the Phoenix*. Rachel Rostad, a poet, rants in her video "To J.K. Rowling, From Cho Chang" about four things. The first thing she rants about is how the non-white characters do not develop throughout the story. She even goes so far as to call the character "worthless" ("Rachel Rostad..."). The second is the way J.K. Rowling stereotyped Cho Chang. Most of the time, when someone hears the word "Asian," they automatically think of the word "nerd." At Hogwarts, the "nerdy" house is Ravenclaw, which coincidentally is the house that Cho Chang belongs to. The next point she brings up is the fact that students of other races make up a minority and that those students are only minor

Hatcher 6

characters in the series whereas the main characters are white. In the video, she states "Between me, Dean, and the Indian twins, Hogwarts has like... five brown people? It doesn't matter we're all minor characters. Nah, you're not racist!" ("Rachel Rostad..."). The last thing she rants about is her name. Cho Chang is a Chinese character whose name is made up of two Korean last names. Rachel Rostad compares this to "a Frenchman being named 'Garcia Sanchez'" ("Rachel Rostad..."). However, this is untrue as "Chang" is actually one of the fifty most common Chinese surnames. Additionally, it is not a fault in the story that the character wasn't developed. Rowling only developed the characters who were essential to the plot. Sure, Cho Chang could have been more developed, but she was only Harry's love interest for two out of seven of the books, so why would she have been?

One more character is often brought up when people start debating whether or not J.K. Rowling is racist. That character is Lavender Brown. In the first few films, where her character is of little significance, she is portrayed as black. Then, comes *Harry Potter and the Half-Blood Prince*. In that book/film, she becomes Ron Weasley's girlfriend. However, she is no longer black. Instead, she is played by a white actress. This does not necessarily mean that J.K. Rowling is racist. If anybody could be considered racist in this situation, it would be the person who selects the cast, because Rowling is not in charge of that, but that is only the case if the casting director did not actually want Lavender to be black. Since interracial relationships are typically looked down upon in today's society, that is semi-understandable. Most of the interracial relationships in movies I have seen are abusive, where the black boyfriend beats up his white girlfriend and goes to jail. Movies like those show interracial relationships in a negative way, corrupting a lot of minds into thinking that they are wrong. So, is that why Lavender Brown jumps from being black to white? Another, more plausible, explanation would just be that they needed a replacement. Maybe the actress that had played her in the first few movies just did not want to be

her anymore, and the casting directors held auditions for a new Lavender. In situations like these, people tend to jump for the racist card rather than thinking through it rationally.

None of these characters make J.K. Rowling a racist. She was trying to create a semi-realistic aspect to her fantasy world. She made most of the students attending Hogwarts white, because the majority of the United Kingdom is white. She did not develop the minor characters because they weren't a part of the bigger picture, not just because they weren't white. That is a pure coincidence. In her novels, she doesn't state whether Lavender is black or white; the casting directors chose the actresses to play her in the movies for any variety of possible reasons.

What J.K. Rowling did was make the wizarding world as realistic as possible by combining fiction with reality. She created an entire fantasy world based on her imagination but integrated so many aspects of the world around her that it came to life for the reader. No one paid attention to the fact that non-white characters were minor characters. They were more interested in the story. As people reread the books as they get older, they notice the race issues that she so cleverly hid in them. She shows us how terrible racism can be in our own world by illustrating how disastrous it is in the wizarding world.

Hatcher 8

Works Cited

Adam. "Did you know Harry Potter was racist." *WordPress*, 21 April 2013, xdind.com/did-you-know-harry-potter-was-racist/.

Bertilsson, Andreas. "Freaks and Muggles: Intolerance and prejudice in *Harry Potter and the Philosopher's Stone*." Kristianstad U., 2007, pp. 3–17.

"Rachel Rostad—'To JK Rowling, from Cho Chang' (CUPSI 2013 Finals)." *YouTube*, uploaded by Button Poetry, 13 April 2013, www.youtube .com/watch?v=iFPWwx96Kew.

Rowling, J.K. *Harry Potter and the Sorcerer's Stone*. Scholastic, 1998.

---. *Harry Potter and the Chamber of Secrets*. Scholastic, 1999.

---. *Harry Potter and the Prisoner of Azkaban*. Scholastic, 1999.

---. *Harry Potter and the Order of the Phoenix*. Scholastic, 2003.

---. *Harry Potter and the Deathly Hallows*. Scholastic, 2007.

Whited, Lana. "1492, 1942, 1992: The Theme of Race in the Harry Potter Series." *The Looking Glass: New Perspectives on Children's Literature*, vol. 10, no. 1, 2006, pp. 1–7.

WILLIAM KAZYAK

William Kazyak was born in Baltimore, MD, but considers his hometown to be Manila, AR. He is an Arkansas State University Piano Performance Major who enjoys playing the piano, listening to classical music and early pop/rock, like the Beach Boys, building model airplanes, and learning about the military. He also enjoys playing sports and running.

Though Kazyak has not always enjoyed writing, he explains, "There have been plenty of times in which what I wanted to say seemed to simply flow out onto the paper. I enjoy being able to put my thoughts down in an orderly manner and being able to refer back to them later."

Kazyak's advice to Composition I and II students? "Good, thoughtful writing takes time—it is not something that can be rushed." He further advises his peers: "Plan the work! Spread it out over time so you are not rushing at the end, and organize it thoughtfully, with smooth transitions from one idea to the next. Take advantage of spare time such as weekends or breaks to think through the assignment and what you want to say."

THE ASSIGNMENT: RESEARCH PAPER

Consider a topic about which you would like to learn more. This topic can be anything, as long as it is a topic appropriate for scholarly inquiry. Students in the past have chosen an historical event, a social or cultural issue, or a scientific theory. Unlike a Researched Argument Paper, which requires you to develop an argumentative thesis, about which reasonable people might disagree, and support that thesis, and that thesis alone, in the body of your paper, a Research Paper asks you to inform yourself and your audience more broadly about the topic.

For this assignment, you will read several primary and secondary sources on your topic. Then, you will share your newly found knowledge in the form of a research paper, integrating scholarly sources into your paper using summary, paraphrase, and quotation. You will need to choose an organization that supports your readers' likely expertise regarding the topic, recognizing that your readers, the A-State University community, are bright and know a lot about many things, but they don't know everything. To this end, you may need to provide background information, identify important concepts and people, and define key terms.

Sample Essay in Chicago Style

William Kazyak

Written for Marcus Tribbett's Composition II Class

· ·

· ·

Note: As you will see, William's essay has been formatted into Chicago style. As is customary in Chicago style, William has included footnotes and a bibliography.

· ·

Deception and Destruction: Operation Fortitude and the Allied Aerial
Support for Operation Overlord

William Kazyak

Composition II

Professor Tribbett

March 29, 2014

1

"We're going in alone, and I don't think we're coming back" rang the words of Wing Commander Josef "Pips" Priller to his wingman, Sergeant Heinz Wodarczyk, on June 6, 1944 with the bleak prospect of their mission. They were embarking on a mission to disrupt, as far as they could, the massive Allied landings on the Normandy beaches. They would be flying into an area infested with hostile aircraft and anti-aircraft guns that would surely shoot them out of the sky before they had a chance to mount an attack. However, Priller and his wingman did make one pass on Sword Beach.[1] It was the only attack made by the German Luftwaffe (air force) on that historic day.[2] The reasons for this have become clear over the decades since D-Day. By June 6, 1944, the Allies had whittled the Luftwaffe down to a mere shadow of its early war glory and gained complete superiority in the skies over Europe.

Air superiority itself, however, did not ensure the success of Operation Overlord. At this point, even without air superiority, the Germans possessed the means for a successful counterattack that could dislodge the allies and throw them back into the sea. The reasons for their lack of appropriate reaction to the invasion stemmed primarily from the fact that the Allies had deceived them concerning the date, location, and force of the invasion through a series of elaborate and ingenious ruses. Code named Operation Fortitude, these efforts, in conjunction with aerial dominance by the Allies, provided critical support to Operation Overlord.

Operation Fortitude was officially put into action on February 23, 1944; less than four months prior to the date of the Overlord landings.[3] Anthony Cave Brown, in his book *Bodyguard of Lies*, gives a very direct and comprehensive statement of the goals of Fortitude. Fortitude was designed to: 1) cause the Germans to make strategic errors by threatening Norway,

---

1. Wynn, *Prelude to Overlord*, 138.

2. McFarland, "Air Combat," 11.

3. Hinsley, "Deception," 174.

2) mislead them concerning the location and date of Overlord, and 3) cause them to make poor strategic decisions after the landings by threatening the Pas de Calais region of France.[4]

The first goal of Operation Fortitude was accomplished by one of its two distinct operations, Fortitude North. Norway was a valuable strategic asset for Germany because it was one of their primary naval bases.[5] Germany had a total of twenty-seven divisions of soldiers stationed in Northwest Europe (including Norway) to guard against an attack there.[6] These soldiers, had they been allowed to be used to reinforce France, could have caused major problems for Overlord, so the Allies had to find a way to keep them in Northwest Europe. Fortunately, Adolf Hitler himself was obsessed with Norway as an asset and was determined to keep it at all costs.[7] This made it relatively easy for the planners of Fortitude North to figure out how to pin down German forces in Norway. In conjunction with the Soviets, the Allies devised a plan to assemble a fake army in Scotland, thereby threatening a two-front invasion. Brown relates the assembly of this army in great detail. In Scotland, the Allies utilized a number of ingenious methods to simulate the build-up of forces of what was supposed to be the British 4th Army Group. The primary method used was bogus radio traffic. A few skilled radio units could move around broadcasting messages to each other that sounded exactly like communications between different units of an army group. This was supplemented by calculated leaks to newspapers, radio, and other press about events supposedly going on involving units in the 4th army. Other methods included placing ships and dummy aircraft in plain view of German recon planes, as well as the purchase of £500,000 of Scandinavian securities by the British; actions that were interpreted by the Germans to mean that an invasion of Northwest Europe was

---

4. Brown, *Bodyguard of Lies*, 460.

5. Penrose, *The D-Day Companion*, 61.

6. Brown, *Bodyguard of Lies*, 460.

7. Ibid., 462.

3

imminent. But the icing on the cake came from agents of Britain's then-secret "XX-Committee," or Double Cross System. XX's agents "Mutt" and "Jeff" both played key roles in Fortitude North by feeding the Germans a mix of false and true information. One of their reports was that Soviet intelligence officer Klementi Budyenny had come to England to discuss the joint invasion of Norway. In reality, Budyenny did come to England, but only to discuss the role the Russians were to play in Fortitude.[8]

Fortitude South was implemented in much the same way as Fortitude North, only it was more involved and played on more of the Germans' pre-dispositions. In the first place, Fortitude South directly threatened an invasion in the Pas de Calais region of France.[9] This part of France was separated from England (specifically Dover) by a mere 25 miles of water.[10] This was the shortest distance between France and England, and the Germans knew this as well as the Allies. The Germans, for their part, built up their strength here, and even stationed the 15th Army, their best soldiers on the Western Front, at Calais.[11] The Allies, for their part, were determined to see to it that those defenses stayed in Calais and were not redeployed to Normandy; at least not until a significant and irreversible build up had occurred.[12] Here again, the Allies turned to bogus armies for this effort. They built-up FUSAG, the First U. S. Army Group, around the command of Lt. General George S. Patton, Jr., an American whom the Germans considered the best Allied commander and expected to lead the invasion.[13] The assembly of FUSAG utilized essentially the same methods as the assembly of 4th Army. Dummy ships, aircraft, tanks and installations as well as calculated press releases and skilled radio operators transmitting build-up

8. Brown, *Bodyguard of Lies*, 464–68.

9. Hinsley, "Deception," 174.

10. Drez, *Voices of D-Day*, 19.

11. Brown, *Bodyguard of Lies*, 461.

12. Penrose, *The D-Day Companion*, 56.

13. Ibid.; Ambrose, "Eisenhower," 267.

4

communications all contributed to the FUSAG scam, and as with the 4th Army deception, XX's agents added further to the confusion. The agents code-named "Garbo" (who was the Germans' most trusted agent) and "Tricycle" played important parts in the scheme, primarily by feeding false information to the Germans.[14]

Fortitude South had one more key aspect: aerial deception. Prior to D-Day, the Allies implemented a strategy to disable as much of the German war effort as possible. This included coastal defenses, airfields, and rail targets.[15] However, if they bombed one area more heavily than the other, the Germans may have deduced the location of the invasion from that strategy. The Allies, therefore, proceeded to attack targets in Calais twice as hard as targets in Normandy in an extension of the effort to make the Germans look to Calais for the invasion.[16] A second role that aircraft played in Fortitude came in a revolutionary new area of warfare: electronic countermeasures. By D-Day, the Allies had developed radar-jamming devices like Window, Moonshine, and Filberts, and had discovered that when properly used in conjunction, they would paint a picture on radar screens of an invasion fleet headed in a certain direction. These methods were perfected and put into practice for D-Day.[17]

The Allies had obviously taken great pains to conceal their true intentions concerning Overlord; now the question was whether or not the Germans would take the bait. *The D-Day Companion*, edited by Jane Penrose, states that Fortitude did not cause the Germans to alter their battle plans; however, this statement is misleading on the surface.[18] According to Brown, the Germans actually reinforced their Norwegian garrisons.[19]

---

14. Brown, *Bodyguard of Lies*, 480–89.

15. Ibid., 521.

16. Penrose, *The D-Day Companion*, 62.

17. Brown, *Bodyguard of Lies*, 524–26.

18. Penrose, *The D-Day Companion*, 63.

19. Brown, *Bodyguard of Lies*, 472.

5

Nevertheless, little response to Fortitude was observed prior to D-Day. It was only after the landings that the staggering success of this astronomical effort was felt. The Germans hesitated to reinforce Normandy for as long as two weeks.[20] Thanks to reports from "Garbo" that Normandy was a fake and FUSAG still planned to invade Calais, the Germans not only failed to reinforce Normandy, but they recalled two Panzer divisions and an infantry division that were already en-route to Normandy and sent them to Calais.[21] The inflated order of battle that "Tricycle" had given the Germans prior to D-Day also came into play by conning the Germans into thinking that most of the Allies' forces were still in England waiting to pounce on Calais the minute they withdrew any forces from there.[22] Overall, Fortitude kept the Germans groping in the dark for the Allies' real intentions until the middle of July, and by that time Allied forces had built-up to the point where it would have been difficult at best to dislodge them.[23]

While this battle of wits was raging, another crucial battle was erupting in the skies over Europe as a prerequisite to D-Day. This was the battle for air superiority. Air superiority had been a major factor in another planned amphibious invasion earlier in the war: Operation Sea Lion, the German plan to invade England.[24] The Germans, however, had not been able to wrest control of the skies over Southern England and the English Channel from the British Royal Air Force, and now they were facing the same challenges that the RAF had met four years earlier. Both the Allies and the Germans knew how crucial air superiority was, and both fought tenaciously for it.

---

20. Budiansky, "The Art of the Double Cross," 44.

21. Ibid.

22. Brown, *Bodyguard of Lies*, 487–99.

23. Penrose, *The D-Day Companion*, 64.

24. Galland, "The First and the Last," 10–16.

6

Dwight D. Eisenhower, the Supreme Allied Commander, had promised his troops prior to D-Day that, "if you see fighting aircraft over you, they will be ours."[25] This bold promise was not an empty one. Since 1943, Allied Bomber crews had been waging a costly war of attrition with the Germans in their attempts to knock out German industry.[26] The arrival of long-range fighter escorts (in particular the P-51 Mustang, which was superior to the German aircraft in nearly every aspect) changed the war entirely.[27] Now it was the Germans who were suffering catastrophic losses, in terms of both pilots and aircraft. At the beginning of 1944, the Germans had 2,395 fighter pilots available for combat, with about half of them actually ready to engage in battle. By the middle of the year, ninety-nine percent of these pilots had been lost.[28] Their aircraft strength had hardly fared better. By D-Day, only forty percent of their total available aircraft (on all fronts) were operable, and on top of that they had pulled the majority of their fighters back to Germany.[29] The German Third Air Force in France was left with around 100 fighters to stop an Allied onslaught of 6,000–7,000 bombers and fighters.[30] Even when the Germans did order their fighters in Germany to head to France, P-51 patrols intercepted and shot down between thirty and fifty percent of them.[31] Those that escaped the dogfights often crashed before reaching their bases due to poor cross country training of the pilots.[32] Fourteen days after the start of the invasion, the German fighter reinforcements were no longer able to fight and were pulled back to Germany.[33]

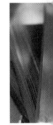

---

25. McFarland, "Air Combat," 12.

26. Wynn, *Prelude to Overlord*, 14.

27. Penrose, *The D-Day Companion*, 118.

28. Ibid., 120–21.

29. Galland, *The First and the Last*, 211; Penrose, *The D-Day Companion*, 117.

30. Galland, *The First and the Last*, 213.

31. McFarland, "Air Combat," 11.

32. Galland, *The First and the Last*, 215.

33. Ibid., 219.

7

While Allied long-range fighters systematically decimated the Luftwaffe, Allied bombers and fighter-bombers were waging an important tactical war to destroy the Germans' ability to reinforce Normandy. The primary aspect of this battle, known as the Transportation Plan, was aimed at obliterating the French Railway system. The Germans relied heavily on this system for movement of troops and especially armored vehicles, such as tanks.[34] Beginning in March, 1944, the Allies pulverized thirty-six rail yards with no less than 139 raids. After May 20, 1944, the juggernaut of the Allied air forces was unleashed against railway bridges and even individual trains. By D-Day, every bridge over the Seine River from Conflans to Rouen, a total of no less than thirty-five crossings, had been reduced to chunks of concrete and steel protruding from the water.[35]

The Transportation Plan effectively neutralized the Germans' ability to reinforce Normandy. The Allies had successfully disabled the Germans' quickest and most effective means of supply and reinforcement. Panzer divisions trying to get to Normandy, now forced to travel under their own power, took anywhere from five days to three weeks to arrive in the battle zone. Even then, their transit was turned into a nightmare as Allied fighter-bombers destroyed anything that moved (tanks were especially prime targets).[36]

On D-Day itself, the Allies made sure that the air over the fleet and the beaches was well covered. During the daytime, P-38 Lightning fighters guarded the shipping lanes between France and England, and when night arrived, the RAF took over the task with a force of night fighters. The beaches were covered by RAF Spitfire fighters down low and by USAAF P-47 Thunderbolt fighters up high. The Allies even added an extra insurance to the landings by sending P-51 Mustangs and more P-38s to form a kill zone further inland with the aim of stopping any German planes long before they

---

34. Ambrose, "Eisenhower," 270.

35. Wynn, *Prelude to Overlord*, 104–6.

36. Penrose, *The D-Day Companion*, 123.

got to the beaches. P-47s and RAF Typhoon fighter-bombers provided close support to the troops by hitting tanks and other vehicles and by neutralizing threats when called upon by the ground forces. Only two Luftwaffe aircraft (the Fw-190 fighters flown by Priller and Wodarczyk) got through to the Allied landing zone; a stunning fulfillment of Eisenhower's promise.[37]

On July 31, 1944, the Allies broke out of Saint-Lô, France, making Overlord an official success.[38] This success, though, came about largely due to the cunning of Allied intelligence officers and the skill and bravery of Allied airmen. Operation Fortitude's stunning success in pinning down German forces elsewhere in Europe and in delaying orders to reinforce Normandy played a major role in buying the Allies the precious time they needed to consolidate their foothold in Europe, and Allied air power supplemented this by destroying both the Luftwaffe and the Germans' means of transportation. Looking back on Overlord, Eisenhower stated that "Without the overwhelming mastery of the air which we attained by that time, our assault on the Continent would have been a most hazardous, if not impossible undertaking," and Adolf Galland, the German Fighter Commander at the time of the invasion, echoes this statement in his book *The First and the Last*.[39] When Priller and Wodarczyk returned to their base after their bold attack on Sword beach, the best they could really do was sit back and look helplessly on as the Third Reich began to crumble under the massive Allied juggernaut; a juggernaut enabled and supported by a brilliant combination of deception and destruction.

---

37. Wynn, *Prelude to Overlord*, 137–38.

38. Galland, *The First and the Last*, 225.

39. Wynn, *Prelude to Overlord*, 26; Galland, *The First and the Last*, 225.

9

Bibliography

Ambrose, Stephen E. "Eisenhower, the Intelligence Community, and the D-Day Invasion." *The Wisconsin Magazine of History* 64, no. 4 (1981): 261–77.

Brown, Anthony Cave. *Bodyguard of Lies.* New York: Harper and Row, Publishers, Inc., 1975.

Budiansky, Stephen. "The Art of the Double Cross." *World War II*, 24, no. 1 (2009): 38–45.

Drez, Ronald J., ed. *Voices of D-Day.* Baton Rouge: Louisiana State University Press, 1994.

Galland, Adolf. *The First and the Last: The Rise and Fall of the German Fighter Forces, 1938–1945,* 2nd ed. Translated by Mervyn Savill. Cutchogue, NY: Buccaneer Books, 1954.

Hinsley, F. H. "Deception." *The D-Day Encyclopedia.* 1994.

McFarland, Stephen L. "Air Combat." *The D-Day Encyclopedia.* 1994.

Penrose, Jane, ed. *The D-Day Companion.* Oxford, United Kingdom: Osprey Publishing, 2004.

Ryan, Cornelius. *The Longest Day: June 6, 1944.* New York: Simon and Schuster, 1959.

Wynn, Humphrey and Susan Young. *Prelude to Overlord: An Account of the Air Operations Which Preceded and Supported Operation Overlord, the Allied Landings in Normandy on D-Day, 6th of June 1944.* Novato, CA: Presidio Press, 1984.

Photo courtesy of William Kazyak

COURTNEY BAKER

Courtney Baker is an avid outdoors-person hailing from Yellville, AR. Courtney enjoys hunting, fishing, kayaking, and camping. She carries this enjoyment of nature into her major in Agricultural Business.

Courtney finds that arranging her thoughts is easier in writing than in speaking. She utilizes an outlining and peer-review process when writing for an assignment. Courtney says that once an outline is in place for a work, "putting it into essay or short-story form is a breeze." When asked specifically about her piece, "Coal Mining: From Providing to Destroying," she credits peer-revision with assisting in finalizing the essay printed here.

Courtney urges her fellow students to have their work reviewed by others. Her initial skepticism of visiting a writing tutor was assuaged when she realized that the tutor helped her "see gaps" in her writing that she "never would have recognized" on her own.

THE ASSIGNMENT: OP-ED

Opposite Editorials or Op-Eds are short, journalistic, argument-driven pieces commonly found in newspapers and online publications. Op-Eds can focus on almost anything: cultural, political, social, humanitarian, educational, or financial issues; particular people, places, or events; or even, another Op-Ed. While informative, an Op-Ed's main purpose is to persuade the reader to see the issue, event, person, or place as the writer does. In fact, some Op-Eds go a step further and, in addition to adding to the readers' previous understanding of the issue also ask for the readers to take action, such as writing a congresswoman a letter or boycotting a restaurant because of its discriminatory practices.

For this assignment, you will write an Op-Ed on a contemporary issue of interest to you. As you begin your paper, consider: what sources and perspectives are missing from the current conversations and media coverage of this topic; what sources, information, and perspectives will add ethos to your argument; and what voice you, the writer, should adopt to best persuade your readers. Keep in mind that the tone and style of an Op-Ed should be dependent on its content, purpose, and audience. Many Op-Eds adopt informal, conversational tones and utilize colloquialisms.

Sample Essay in APA Style

Courtney Baker

Written for Marcus Tribbett's Composition II Class

· ·

· ·

Note: As you will see, Courtney's essay has been formatted into APA style. As is customary in APA style, Courtney has not included signal phrases throughout her piece where she has integrated sources. Instead, she has included only the in-text citation.

· ·

Running head: COAL MINING   1

Coal Mining: From Providing to Destroying

Courtney Baker

Arkansas State University

Coal Mining: From Providing to Destroying

Coal mining in the Appalachian Mountains of West Virginia seems as natural as the abundant forest that covers the land. For many years these hills have provided the United States with its primary source of electricity—coal. Recently, however, tides have changed in the coal mining industry, bringing a new method of mining that is leaving West Virginians in a heated debate. It is called Mountaintop Removal Valley-Fill Mining (MRVF). This process involves blowing the top off of a mountain using dynamite and then "stripping" the seams of coal that lay exposed after the blast (Geller, 2009). The efficiency of this act has been out-weighed by its perceived stigma, and the controversy that surrounds it sees no end in sight. Ultimately, as is revealed in the informative documentary *Coal Country*, MRVF is the center point in an argument that is less about the method and more about money, beliefs, and long-standing ways of life (Geller, 2009).

One of the initial rationales for developing MRVF was its potential to save money. As opposed to underground mining, surface mining does not require near as many workers (Geller, 2009). Therefore, the mining companies are obligated to pay far fewer employees, which is where the companies see the bulk of their savings. Additionally, without the use of underground mining tunnels, there are far fewer safety precautions that must be met. Being able to extract coal without having to build safe tunneling for employees allows companies to cut safety costs and ship out coal even quicker than before. Thus, MRVF is less costly and more efficient, which leads directly to increased profit.

The question remains though, if MRVF is so cheap and efficient, why isn't it the universally preferred mining method? This is because while MRVF is profitable for the mining companies, it has not been profitable for the workers. This is illustrated through the mining district in West Virginia, which is no longer seeing profit from its rich resources. The money being made from the region's coal is being monopolized strictly within the mining companies (Geller, 2009). Because of this, communities in the mining hills are quickly fading, many workers have lost their jobs, and many of the towns are now ghost towns with only a few faithful citizens. These once-thriving mining communities provide the majority of our country's electricity, yet the people that live there are now struggling to get by while the mining companies are making record profits.

Further opposition to MRVF comes from those who find that it conflicts with their values such as conservationists. Conservationists are leading contenders in the fight against surface mining because it destroys so much of the Appalachian mountain range. When the miners remove the mountaintops, the mountains are gone forever. Proponents of MRVF, such as the mining companies who utilize this method, argue that they "reclaim" the mountain after they are done. This involves spreading the discarded rock back along the mining site to resurface the location as best they can (Geller, 2009). This may technically be true, but these reclamation sites are easily distinguished from the rest of the forest because they do not allow for comparable diverse vegetative growth. Environmental advocates are fighting for the preservation of the mountains and the forests that thrive on them. The miners and the mining companies, however, see it a little differently, believing that, as long as the mountain is there and the coal is inside, they have the right to harvest it and use it to their benefit.

Somewhere in the middle of this debate are the coal miners, many of who want to mine the way they always have, the way their fathers did, and the way their fathers' fathers did. They argue that mining has been a way of life for hundreds of years and that without coal mining, the communities present in places like Appalachia, West Virginia will be literally nonexistent.

COAL MINING   4

In the end, MRVF is more efficient and less costly for the coal mining companies, but at what cost to the mining communities and the environment? The costs to coal miners, citizens of mining districts, and the environment are grave and many. By cutting jobs, and destroying and polluting the land, MRVF and the coal mining companies are not helping preserve coal mining heritage or the environment, they are destroying them, and, ultimately, only helping themselves.

Reference

Geller, P. (Director & Producer). (2009). *Coal Country* [Motion picture]. United States: Evening Star Productions.

An Introduction to the Promise and Perils of Primary Research

By Kristi Murray Costello

Inspired by the part of David Bartholomae's article, "Inventing the University," in which he discusses the sheer rhetorical adaptability we ask students to possess, such as writing for anthropology, history, chemistry, biology, and Writing Studies all in the same semester, I consider again the standard research paper, its typical decontextualization, and the ways in which we ask undergraduate students to mimic being "members of the academy, or historians or anthropologists or economists," but how seldom we create assignments that allow them to actually be part of the academy and experience what it means to be a scholar (5).

In his book, *Rhetoric at the Margins*, David Gold writes that in 1930 Arkansas State University was the site of one of the first interracial debates in the U.S. (46). The debate was with Wiley College, which was led by the famous Melvin Tolson (subject of the movie, *The Great Debaters*). Gold explains, "That a team from a small black college could travel so widely—much less successfully—during the height of the Depression is a remarkable achievement" (46).

Wanting to know more about this event, this time in history, and the role of Arkansas State University, my undergraduate Advanced Composition students and I worked together last spring to uncover as much information as we could about the debate as well as the region, the university, and race relations of the time through archival work, research, and interviews. We learned about the price of meat (10¢ per pound) and that lynchings of people of color, mostly men, were public and described in the local newspaper. Sources showed us that money was tight and racial tensions were high. Interestingly, we also discovered that the debate in 1930 actually happened at Arkansas State (short for Arkansas State College for Negroes), which was the common designation for AM&N, the state's first HBCU (Historically Black College or University), now University of Arkansas Pine Bluff ("Arkansas State and Wiley College Debate"). Rae, Lathan, Colby, and Meagan further discovered through searching newspapers that ASU-Pine Bluff and Wiley College faced off again just a year later in Hot Springs to a packed crowd ("Arkansas State and Wiley College Debate"); another group discovered that the two teams faced off again in 1936 to debate world peace "Debate Peace at Arkansas State"). Though our evidence is still somewhat flimsy on this, it looks like Arkansas State University, as we know it, and Wiley College faced off years later, just after desegregation, which would suggest that while A-State Jonesboro did not participate in Wiley's (and the nation's) first round of interracial debates, they were not far behind.

This project allowed the students the opportunity not to act as writers, historians, and researchers, but to *be* writers, historians, and researchers. This project also taught students about their community, how to collaborate effectively, and how to work with others on campus and in the community to gather information. As you will see in Rae, Lathan, Colby, and Meagan's paper, it also helped students experience firsthand the elation and tribulations of primary research.

Works Cited

"Arkansas State and Wiley College Debate." *The Chicago Defender* (National Edition), 11 Apr. 1931, ezproxy.library.astate.edu/login?url=https://search.proquest.com/docview/492312147?accountid=8363. Accessed 10 May 2017.

Bartholomae, David. "Inventing the University." *Journal of Basic Writing*, no. 1, 1986, p. 4. *EBSCOhost*, ezproxy.library.astate.edu/login?url=http://search.ebscohost.com/login.aspx?direct=true&db=edsjsr&AN=edsjsr.43443456&site=eds-live.

"Debate Peace at Arkansas State." *The Chicago Defender* (National Edition), 25 July 1936, ezproxy.library.astate.edu/login?url=https://search.proquest.com/docview/492518037?accountid=8363. Accessed 10 May 2017.

Gold, David. *Rhetoric at the Margins: Revising the History of Writing Instruction in American Colleges, 1873–1947.* Southern Illinois University Press, 2008, pp. 27–45.

Primary Research

Collaborative Scholarly Investigation and Project Overview

Kristi Murray Costello

Advanced Composition, Spring 2016

OVERVIEW

David Gold alleges that in 1930 Arkansas State University was the site of one of the first interracial debates in the U.S. Together, my class and I learned about this debate, research methods, and scholarly writing. And in doing so, as David Bartholomae suggested, we became "insiders" and "work[ed] and participate[d] in a common enterprise" (10–11).

LOGISTICS

The class was divided into four groups and each group was assigned to learn about their particular method well enough, through practice and research, to teach the class.

THE PREPARATION

- **Group 1: INTERNET AND DATABASES SEARCH**: Search the internet and articles from online databases about the debate, the time period, Wiley college, Arkansas State University (hint: then it was called Arkansas State College), and related topics (including Works Cited pages of articles). Be ready to discuss the following questions: Where did you search? What search terms did you use? Where did these searches take you? Be sure to focus on methods, ethics, and tips, process, and findings. Talk to our resource librarian and help develop ideas and tips for other groups' searches.

- **Group 2: NEWSPAPERS AND MICROFICHE**: Check our school and local newspapers, and see if you can access Wiley's school and local newspapers. You might even find it helpful to look at regional and national papers to get a sense of the time period. Engage in internet research about how to search, talk to someone at the library about how to search newspapers, and be ready to share this information with your classmates—does all of the equipment work? Do you have to have appointments? Are there some searches the online newspaper works better for and others it doesn't?

- **Group 3: ARCHIVAL WORK including A-State yearbooks**: Look through our university's archives, and any other materials that may be helpful, here and at Wiley (you'll see that they have some archival information online). Also, check the references in "Rhetoric on the Margins." Engage in internet research to see what sites have which materials, talk to professors and/or archivalists about ethics of working with this information, how to find it, etc.

- **Group 4: INTERVIEWS**: Interview people who may know something about the debate and/or debate team here, or elsewhere. Also interview at least one historian who can tell you about the time period, particularly in this region. You should conduct at least four interviews. Think outside the box. Engage in internet research and talk to professors about appropriate interviewing strategies.

The Presentation (25–30 minutes)

Your group will teach the rest of the class **how to conduct your assigned method/s, tips for doing so effectively and efficiently here at A-State and in general, and the ethics of doing so.** You will need to walk your classmates through your process, including who you talked to, what worked, what didn't, what you had access to, what you didn't, etc. You will need to research your method/s through practice, talking to experts, such as librarians and professors, and reading outside sources. All of your practice should entail trying to uncover details about the debate at A-State in 1930, or related information (like what else was going on around that time). In addition to presenting your assigned method, you will also *present your results (or lack thereof) to the class*. Keep in mind that the results are only *one* part of your presentation. Be mindful of the fact that sometimes what you don't find is just as important as what you do find and, for this project, learning about the method (and articulating what you learned with your classmates) is just as, if not more important, than the information itself.

The Project (4–6 page group paper in MLA format)

You should have an argument, theme, or main idea that ties this together as a cohesive paper. Then, we will work together as a class to merge the group papers into one scholarly article.

- Introduction (about 1 page)
- Methods: What did you learn about your method in terms of best practices, access, and ethics? What steps did you take? Tell us about your research process. (about 1½ page)
- Findings: What did you find? What did you learn about the method AND the debate/time in history? (about 1½ page)
- Conclusion (about 1 page)

Primary Research

Primary Research

Raiders of the Lost Archives:
Researching the 1930 Arkansas v. Wiley College Debate

Rae Summers-Thompson, Colby Cockrill, Lathan Garnett, and Meagan Hamilton

In 1930, Melvin B. Tolson led the historically black Wiley College in what would become a ten-year winning streak against Southern college debate teams. Initiating the first interracial debate ever in the South, Wiley College took on Oklahoma City University and ended with the University of Southern California, hitting several schools along the way. The Wiley College Debate Team defeated every college they went up against (Beil). According to David Gold in his book, *Rhetoric at the Margins*, Wiley College also debated Arkansas State University (ASU) the same year (46). With this in mind, we, students in Dr. Kristi Costello's Advanced Composition class at Arkansas State University, made it our goal to discover all that we can about this momentous occasion and important time in our region's history. That being said, while today we celebrate the Wiley College debaters for their role in what was a huge step in the promotion of racial equality in North America, factors including racial bias, the Great Depression, and a devastating fire on our campus, left very little information regarding Arkansas State University's early debate teams and Wiley College's trials and tribulations as they traveled down America's southern roads.

In an endeavor to increase the amount of information that could be found, Dr. Costello's class was separated into four groups: interviews, archives, newspapers and microfiche, and internet and online databases. This section of the report contains the archival group's research methods throughout the project, as well as any findings collected through those research methods. Our group also employed other methodologies of research in order to determine direction of archival research.

METHOD

Our journey began with archives and the goal of uncovering material on the Wiley College debate against Arkansas State College. To this end, first, we decided that we should look in the physical archives on the seventh floor of the Arkansas State University library. We quickly learned that it has its own set of rules: one must sign in, researchers may have a pencil (no pens) and a piece of paper—no electronic devices, and no backpacks or purses. Additionally, materials that a researcher wishes to view must be requested, and those materials may only be viewed in the designated room. Observing all of the strict rules, we looked through the 1930 Arkansas State University ASU yearbook, *The Yearling*, which led us to learning that

Arkansas State was then called First District Agricultural and Mechanical College or A&M College, for short, and became Arkansas State College in 1933. We started by going to the section marked, "Clubs and Activities." Next, we read through the information listed beside every senior's picture, looking to find any individual members of the debate team.

Following an attempt to search the archives at the Craighead Historical Society and after scouting through the online archives, found through Google, we turned our attention to the online newspaper databases, having learned that archival research is not only limited to physical preserved items. There are digital archives that often store valuable photographs, advertisements, and newspaper articles. While in the Arkansas State University ASU archives, we attempted to view the digital archives of the *Herald*, the college newspaper, and sorted through *Historical Newspapers*. It takes time to go through various search terms and even more time searching through the abundance of newspaper articles from the 1930s, but patience may return rich rewards.

Our first step searching online newspaper databases was to go to www. astate.edu/library. On the Arkansas State University ASU Library's home page, there is a link that says, "All Library Databases." Once we clicked on the link, we changed the *database type* to "News" in the drop down menu, which displays all the news databases. We then scrolled down to the "H" section and clicked on "Historical Newspapers." Then we typed the search term, "Wiley College." After the results were up, we changed the publication dates, which are located on the left side of the page, to 1930–1939. Satisfied with the articles that made the cut, we scrolled through them in search of something that mentions Arkansas State College and Wiley College. Lastly, we read through the resulting articles with hope of uncovering something that would help us in our journey to find what happened during that debate and glimpses into the time period.

Through conducting archival research, we learned that it is important to be imaginative and to pay attention to every detail, because things that may seem minor have the potential of leading to a more major discovery. We also learned that, when using newspaper or digital archives, it is important to know exact or close approximate dates of the information being sought. Having learned this, we now also know that preliminary research as well as an attempt to acquire necessary resources will help the research process. More broadly, we learned that the degree of successful archival research depends on several factors: it depends on diligent and faithful preservation of documents, photographs, books, and other memorabilia; the preserved materials must be stored in a place that resists destruction (fires, floods, etc.); one must have access (which might depend on time, mobility, and financial resources) to the archived materials in need.

Primary Research

FINDINGS

The dual objectives of this project, to find information regarding a debate between Arkansas and Wiley colleges in 1930 and learn about conducting primary archival research, were resolved more so in the latter methods than in the former. Due to a popular Hollywood film, *The Great Debaters*, which was produced by Oprah Winfrey and directed by and starred Denzel Washington, there is information available (predominantly online and in the Wiley College archives) about the Wiley College debate team. We found the names and photographs of their team members and their coach, Melvin Tolson, on the website *The Great Debaters*. We also found information regarding several other colleges Wiley debated that year, including Arkansas State University–Pine Bluff, but not specifically Arkansas State A&M College. Realities regarding the social and economic climate of the period possibly contributed to the lack of publicity of the debate.

ARCHIVES

We used Google to find and access digital archives from the region, such as Arkansas State University's own History and Heritage, which we cite throughout this piece. In fact, it was through these digital archives, we learned about the "major fire [that] consumed the Administration/ Classroom Building in the early morning hours of Jan. 12, 1931, the first day of spring semester classes," which may have led to a lack of materials regarding the debate team (History & Heritage).

We also looked at a physical copy of Arkansas's 1930 yearbook, the *Yearling*, in which there is no mention of a debate team. The title page in the yearbook records the name of what is currently Arkansas State University as then being the State Agricultural and Mechanical College. There are no newspapers, files, photographs, or any other source of information in the Arkansas State University archives pertaining to the 1930 debates. Likewise, we could not find any materials with the Craighead Historical Society. On the other hand, we did find some books that include information about Melvin B. Tolson, the debate team's founder and coach, as well as reviews of his written work (Flasch; Lenhardt). However, there was no information to be found in the books regarding any 1930 debates with Arkansas.

INTERVIEWS

We interviewed Dr. Brady Banta, the Associate Director of Arkansas State University archives and faculty member of the Heritage Studies Ph.D. Program. Dr. Banta informed us that there had been a fire in the administration building of the university that would have destroyed any possible materials, including any and all records dating from 1928 to 1932. He also taught us about the social and economic conditions of Jonesboro in 1930. He explained to us that Craighead County, home of Arkansas State University (ASU), was a predominantly agricultural region. Perhaps the most helpful information from the interview was that Arkansas College was segregated in 1930, and it remained so until the 1960s, making it unlikely that the two schools met publically in the 1930s. If a debate had happened, it was likely that it was not reported to the newspaper for fear of repercussion. Dr. Banta also very graciously offered to comb through a collection of which he told us had belonged to the first principal of ASU, Dr. Kay. Unfortunately, Dr. Banta reported that he could not find anything related to the debates.

We also attempted to gain interviews with Wiley College and author Gary Lenhardt, but received no response to emails.

INTERNET AND DATABASES

We anticipated that the group assigned to Internet and Databases would exhaust the information that could be found on popular search engines, like Google, so we first gravitated toward published newspapers, which we expected might have been likely to report on community events, such as college debates. In particular, Dr. Banta suggested we explore the database, Historical Newspapers (our process is detailed above). Next, we searched Google and, through it, learned additional information about the social and economic climate of the 1930s. Lynchings were not only an acceptable practice in the South, but were the common mode of punishment for any person of color who was accused of any offense (Shipman). Because this area consisted largely of farmers and sharecroppers, the Great Depression in 1930 critically impacted numerous people and businesses (Arkansas State University). Interestingly, though people and banks alike were being foreclosed and going bankrupt, Arkansas College actually grew (History & Heritage).

Primary Research

While there is evidence available regarding debates between the two colleges later than 1930, we have naught but rumor and speculation concerning a debate between the two in that specific year. We may also speculate that, due to Jim Crowism and the bigoted ideals that supported those laws, publicity of an interracial debate would have been undesired. Not only would an interracial debate have been distasteful and controversial to many during an already volatile period, but, due to those very reasons, publicizing such an event could have proven dangerous for all those involved. Additionally, as far as news coverage went, debate matches were not considered sellable stories; in other words, it was not common practice to publish news stories about intercollegiate debates, regardless of race.

CONCLUSION

Our team did locate evidence that supports that Wiley College debated Arkansas State University Pine Bluff in 1931 at a tournament in Hot Springs in a newspaper article found within the Historical Newspapers databases titled, "Arkansas State and Wiley College Debate." The article never mentioned Pine Bluff so we can see how scholars, such as Gold, may have been confused (see the postscript for an additional curveball). And, how exciting to aid in better illuminating history. Because of this and our new-found experience with and appreciation of research, we call this research project a success.

We started with little information about the debate, questioning the actual event itself. Through our research, we learned more about our university's rich history, past race relations in our region, and we have even been able to determine that the teams did meet at a later date than the suspected first debate at a neutral location, in Hot Springs, AR, housing multitudes beyond expectations. This is evidence that Wiley College did, in fact, draw attention to their debates. Additionally, we can see that Wiley obviously traveled many miles and this information sheds light on the existence of traveling teams, in general, which means that a debate between the two teams did not necessarily take place at Arkansas State College. In our research we have seen that there are various theories as to why the city of Jonesboro, Arkansas, home of Arkansas State College, would not publish information about this debate even if it had happened. At this time, there were social class issues, such as the Great Depression and segregation under Jim Crow laws, which influenced the mindset of many American citizens. The debaters' safety had to be taken into account in regards to both parties. Since lynchings were so common, we can assume that African American students in a rural Southern town were not welcomed with open arms.

As we researched, we witnessed that different types of research are best for different research topics. For example, for this debate that happened in

1930, with very little information publicized by local news, interviews were not a very good avenue of research. All of the people involved in the actual debate are now passed away, any people that would have been young during that time are also probably no longer around, or they did not realize the importance of the event as it happened. Archives and microfiche seemed to be promising avenues, although they both provided little information. Contrary to our assumptions, internet databases were challenging for finding reliable sources and specific information about the debate.

Primary research has proved to us that this practice is many degrees different from secondary research. In primary research we are responsible for the information we gather, and we are responsible for finding reliable resources. This research is unlike most of the research many students conduct; in secondary research there have been previous researchers to compile information. When we are the first researchers, we cannot pull from previously compiled information, because *we* are the ones compiling this information. This is an exciting privilege and should be taken seriously. Further, primary research is a difficult job to undertake and takes skill, hard work, imagination, attention to even the smallest details, and patience. That being said, it should also be mentioned that there is a great deal of excitement and satisfaction in the process itself. Creating theories and tracking down details can be both challenging and exhilarating. Such a journey can take a passive student researcher and turn her into an active investigator.

POST-SCRIPT, WRITTEN BY RAE SUMMERS-THOMPSON

Since submitting this project, Smithsonian's National Museum of African American History & Culture published a new website. In it, one may view two pages of Henrietta Bell Wells's, one of Wiley's most notable debate alums, scrapbook. The second of these pages contains pressed flowers as souvenirs of her travels. Upon magnifying the page to examine her handwriting, one may see that she has written, "And this is a flower that I stole from Arkansas State College at my very first debate." Scholarly articles, however, suggest that Wiley College's first interracial debate at a Southern venue was in Oklahoma City, so this finding stirs up more questions. Did *she* debate in OK City? If not, did Wiley College, in fact, travel to Arkansas State College for a debate that year, or did they perhaps stop at the campus at some point for some unknown reason? It has been rumored that Tolson, Wiley's coach, was attempting to unionize share croppers in this area. Perhaps while here the two teams defied all odds and went toe to toe in an exchange of ideas. Only further research will tell....

Works Cited

"Arkansas State and Wiley College Debate." *The Chicago Defender* (National Edition), 11 Apr. 1931, ezproxy.library.astate.edu/login?url=https://search.proquest.com/docview/492312147?accountid=8363. Accessed 10 May 2017.

"Arkansas State University (ASU)." *Encyclopedia of Arkansas History and Culture.* The Central Arkansas Library System, 2016, encyclopediaofarkansas.net/encyclopedia/entry-detail.aspx?entryID=2374. Accessed 23 Mar. 2016.

Banta, Brady. Personal interview. 11 Mar. 2016.

Beil, Gail. "Wiley College's Great Debaters." *Humanities Texas.* Feb. 2008, humanitiestexas.org/news/articles/wiley-colleges-great-debaters. Accessed 15 Mar. 2016.

Flasch, Joy. *Melvin B. Tolson.* Twayne Publishers, 1972.

Gold, David. *Rhetoric at the Margins: Revising the History of Writing Instruction in American Colleges, 1873–1947.* Southern Illinois University Press, 2008, pp. 27–45.

"History & Heritage." Arkansas State University, n.d. www.astate.edu/info/about-asu/history/. Accessed 18 March 2016.

Lenhart, Gary. *The Stamp Of Class: Reflections On Poetry And Social Class.* University of Michigan Press, 2006.

Shipman, Marlin. "Forgotten Men and Media Celebrities: Arkansas Newspaper Coverage of Condemned Delta Defendants in the 1930s." *Arkansas Review: A Journal of Delta Studies,* Aug 2000, Vol. 31 Issue 2, p. 110. D.umn.edu, nd. Accessed 21 Mar. 2016.

The Great Debaters. The Great Debaters/Wiley College, 2015. Accessed 9 Mar. 2016.

The Yearling. State Agricultural and Mechanical College, 1930.

The Great Debaters. Directed by Denzel Washington, performances by Denzel Washington, Nate Parker, Jurnee Smollett-Bell. Harpo, 2007.